Trust in the LORD with all your heart and lean not on your own understanding; in all your ways submit to him, and he will make your paths straight.

—Proverbs 3:5–6 (NIV)

MYSTERIES *of* BLACKBERRY VALLEY

Where There's Smoke
The Key Question
Seeds of Suspicion
A Likely Story
Out of the Depths
Run for the Roses
Crooks and Christmas Cookies
Smoke and Mirrors
No Love Lost
The Cookbook Clue
The Final Cut
A Brush with Danger
The Mandolin Mystery
Forged in Fire

the community. And Hannah had quickly learned that any size and scale of wedding involved an abundance of choices.

Hannah leaned against the hostess stand. "Though this week I'll be spending more time getting ready for Lacy's baby shower than I will be doing things for the wedding."

Elaine clapped her hands together, her dark brown eyes shining. "I still can't believe how close the Minyards are to having their baby."

Hannah grinned so hard her cheeks hurt. She'd never been so excited to throw a party. Every time she thought about snuggling her best friend's newborn baby, a thrill ran through her. Hannah loved babies, and she loved Lacy and Neil, so this was as exciting as the anticipated arrivals of her niece and nephews years before.

"I'm so excited that I might have been too ambitious planning the food for Sunday," she said with a chuckle. "It's hard for me to restrain myself when it comes to themed food."

"What's the theme?"

"The farm." Lacy owned and operated Bluegrass Hollow Farm, which supplied fresh eggs to the Hot Spot as well as to plenty of other customers.

"That's perfect," Elaine said. "Do you want some extra help?"

Hannah waved away the offer. "You don't need to do that."

"I know, but I want to. What if I take care of the decorating so you can focus on the food?"

Hannah hesitated. She'd always been much better at offering help to others than she was at accepting it.

"Please?" Elaine persisted. "I love decorating, and you have enough to do with getting the food ready. Let me help."

"We don't make it into Blackberry Valley as often as we'd like." Rusty slid his laptop into his bag and stood. "Our house is in the country, but Cave City is a bit closer, so that's where we typically end up when we need groceries or a quick bite to eat. They don't have anything like the Hot Spot there, though."

"Did Pamela grow up in Blackberry Valley as well?"

"Nope, just me." Rusty slung the strap of his bag over his shoulder and gazed out the tall, wide front windows of the Hot Spot. "I like where we live, but I do miss being in town sometimes. Still feels like home when I'm here."

Hannah followed his gaze out to Main Street. Today was the seventh of July, and the Americana banners and decorations from the annual Fourth of July celebration still lined the street. Despite the heat and humidity, July was a picturesque month in Blackberry Valley, with flowers in bloom and the trees a vibrant green.

Hannah and Rusty exchanged warm farewells and then he was gone, taking with him one of the most dreaded recurring tasks on her to-do list. She couldn't stop smiling.

"Good meeting?" asked Elaine Wilby, the Hot Spot hostess.

"Fantastic. I think he's going to be a huge help."

Elaine grinned and tucked her dark hair behind her ears. "I like hearing that. Now that you're running the Hot Spot plus planning a wedding, I've been a little worried about your stress level."

"Me too," Hannah admitted.

She had imagined planning a wedding would feel romantic and exciting—and it did sometimes, but it also felt overwhelming. Even though neither she nor Liam wanted an elaborate celebration, it was hard to plan something "simple" when they both had deep roots in work, but you've done a fine job keeping up with it. You'd be surprised how many small business owners have called me in a panic, and I find they've never recorded a single thing."

Hannah felt a touch of pride at Rusty's compliment. He reminded her of her father in many ways, though Rusty was probably only in his fifties. But, like sixtysomething Gabriel Prentiss, Rusty was generous with compliments and laughter. And when he smiled, his eyes crinkled in the same way as her dad's.

Raquel Holden materialized at the table, holding a to-go box and wearing her usual warm smile. "Here's that fried chicken salad for you, sir. Anything else I can get for either of you?"

Hannah smiled at her friend and server, whom she'd had the privilege of employing for over a year now. Raquel's black curls were pulled back into a jaunty ponytail that suited her well, and she wore a touch of shimmery eye makeup that made her dark eyes seem even livelier than usual. "Nothing for me. Thanks, Raquel."

"Me neither," Rusty said.

Raquel headed for a table of newly seated guests perusing their menus.

Rusty tapped the to-go box. "My wife will be thrilled. Thank you so much. You're sure I can't pay for it?"

Hannah shook her head, sending her blond hair swaying. "Not a chance. This meeting has taken a huge weight off my shoulders."

"I'll be a hero when I walk in the door holding this. Pamela told me she had a dream about this salad last night. That's how much she loves it."

"It's our most popular salad this summer. I think it's the candied bacon."

Chapter One

The longer Hannah Prentiss sat at the table with bookkeeper Rusty Studebaker, the lighter her heart felt. Why had she waited so long to get help with managing the Hot Spot's finances?

Both her fiancé, Liam Berthold, and her best friend, Lacy Minyard, had been telling her that she should outsource this part of owning a restaurant. Lacy had gone so far as to share stories about how much more relaxed her husband, Neil, was since he'd hired Rusty. Finally, Hannah had agreed to meet with him, and now she couldn't believe she'd put this off for so long. While neither Liam nor Lacy were likely to say, "I told you so," Hannah wouldn't blame either of them if they did.

As Rusty wrapped up his explanation of the best way for Hannah to scan and send him receipts, she released an intentionally dramatic sigh. "Rusty, I think you're an answer to prayer."

He chuckled. "I'll have to tell my mother you said that. She wanted me to go into ministry. I'm not sure she's ever believed that accounting can be the Lord's work too."

Hannah sipped at her sweet tea. "I'm certainly glad He gifted you with numbers, because that's not the way He gifted me."

"You're being too hard on yourself." Rusty popped a french fry into his mouth. Hannah was sure that by now it was too cold to be any good, but he didn't complain. "You may not enjoy bookkeeping

Forged in Fire

Published by Guideposts
100 Reserve Road, Suite E200
Danbury, CT 06810
Guideposts.org

Cover and interior design by Müllerhaus
Cover illustration by Bob Kayganich at Illustration Online LLC.
Typeset by Aptara, Inc.

ISBN 978-1-965859-14-8 (hardcover)
ISBN 978-1-965859-15-5 (softcover)
ISBN 978-1-965859-16-2 (epub)

Printed and bound in the United States of America
10 9 8 7 6 5 4 3 2 1

MYSTERIES *of* BLACKBERRY VALLEY

Forged in Fire

STEPHANIE COLEMAN

Guideposts

The shower was happening a few hours after church in her apartment above the Hot Spot, and a set of extra hands would be nice.

"If you're sure you don't mind..." Hannah hedged.

"Are you kidding? Decorating for a baby shower is a delight. What time do you want me here?"

"Maybe twelve thirty? The shower starts at two."

Elaine pulled her phone from her pocket. "I'm putting it in my calendar now. Do I need to pick up decorations, or did you already buy some?"

"Everything has been purchased. I'm not sure how long the actual decorating will take, but I'm sure there will be plenty to do. Thank you so much, Elaine."

"Thanks for letting me help."

Elaine put her phone away as the doors opened. A young couple came inside, holding hands and gazing dreamily at each other.

Elaine smiled at them as she gathered menus. "Welcome to the Hot Spot. Table for two?"

Hannah's phone buzzed in her back pocket, but she waited until Elaine had led the couple away before she pulled it out to check who was calling. She'd anticipated the call being from Liam, who'd left that morning along with his best friend and fellow firefighter, Archer Lestrade, to help with raging wildfires in Wyoming. Hannah was so proud of them for voluntarily heading up there to help, but saying goodbye that morning had felt harder than she'd anticipated.

She blinked a few times at the screen, which didn't say *Liam "My Favorite Fiancé" Berthold*, but instead read *Aunt Fiona*. Fiona Western was her mother's younger sister, and while she sent occasional emails and texts, Hannah couldn't remember the last time she'd received a phone call from her. Was something wrong?

Hannah swiped to answer the call. "Hello?" she asked in a slightly breathless voice as she stepped outside into the soupy afternoon heat.

"Hannah!" Aunt Fiona's high-pitched voice sounded chipper, not distressed. "I wasn't sure if you'd be able to answer your phone during business hours."

"You caught me at a good time, fortunately. Though I did assume something was wrong when I saw you were calling."

Aunt Fiona laughed. "Isn't that sad? We all think the worst when we get phone calls these days. How is my favorite restaurateur doing? Is that the right term?"

"You nailed it. I'm good." Hannah considered the potted geraniums Elaine had arranged outside the Hot Spot, and pinched off a dead flower. "Maybe a little busier than I'd like to be, but I've never been great at sitting still. How are you?"

"Even as a girl, you were always very busy. I remember one visit when you served me constant cups of pretend tea. Cherry tea, cinnamon tea, grape tea—on and on." Aunt Fiona's voice took on a wistful tone. "Frieda and I laughed and laughed about it. Those were good days."

Hannah wished she could remember serving pretend tea to her mom and her aunt, but her memories didn't stretch back that far. However, she remembered well the joy she always felt as a child when she heard Aunt Fiona was coming for a visit. Her mother's sister didn't come often, but she always arrived ready to have fun.

"That's actually related to why I'm calling," Aunt Fiona continued. Her voice had the same husky tone that Hannah's did whenever she was fighting off tears. "I turn fifty-six next week, and it has me thinking about Frieda almost constantly. I'll be turning the same age as my big sister, and it's strange to think that before long I'll be older than she was. That makes this birthday feel very significant, and I'd like to spend it at home in Blackberry Valley."

"We would love to have you." Hannah's insides fizzed with the anticipation of seeing her mother's only sister again. "You can stay with me."

"You're sure it wouldn't be too much trouble?"

"Of course not. When would you arrive?"

"Is Friday too soon? If I leave DC after breakfast, I could be in Blackberry Valley by dinnertime."

"Friday would be perfect." Hannah couldn't stop grinning. "Aunt Fiona, I'm so excited."

"I am too. I haven't seen you or Gabriel or any of my high school friends in far too long."

Hannah often felt it had been too long since she'd seen Aunt Fiona. Her aunt was one of the coolest people she knew. As a nurse, she'd lived all over the United States. She had the best stories, the prettiest clothes, and the heartiest laugh. How strange that she seemed so much younger than Hannah's mother, but was about to turn the same age Mom had been when she'd succumbed to cancer. Hannah had always thought that fifty-six was far too young to die, and the older she got, the truer that seemed.

After saying goodbye, Hannah headed back into the Hot Spot. Just that morning, she'd been thinking how quiet July might feel after Lacy's baby shower. With the Fourth of July festivities over, Liam out of town being his wonderful heroic self, and the next menu change for the Hot Spot still weeks away, Hannah had foreseen lots of time alone at her apartment, working on wedding plans.

But with Aunt Fiona coming to town, there was no chance that life in Blackberry Valley would feel "quiet" at all.

Chapter Two

There was nothing like the impending arrival of company to make a person notice tasks they'd been putting off for far too long.

With bright midmorning light streaming through her apartment windows, Hannah stared at the pile of nine boxes in the corner of her living room. Her dad had been cleaning out some rooms at the house he shared with his brother, Gordon, and he'd come across these boxes that belonged to her. A few were left over from childhood, but several were from Hannah's move back to Blackberry Valley. She'd stashed quite a few at her dad's place while renovation work was being done, and she thought she'd retrieved all of them, but apparently not. Dad had discovered and delivered them last week, and before Hannah hosted the baby shower or her aunt, she needed to take care of them.

She considered the boxes, debating which one she should start with—and promptly walked to the kitchen to refill her coffee instead.

"You can't keep stalling," Hannah muttered into her fresh, steaming cup. "It's just nine boxes. Let's get this done."

Plus, the timing was perfect. Grace Community Church was currently collecting donations for a church garage sale to raise money for a missionary couple they supported in Uganda. Not only could Hannah clean out her living space, she could also donate to a good cause. Considering she'd forgotten these existed, surely she didn't need most of the things they contained.

She pulled the first one off the pile, opened the flaps, and stared inside. Grief formed a lump in her throat. The box was full of scrapbooks that her mom had put together. Mom loved scrapbooking and had continued to work at it until her final weeks of life. Hannah had space on her bookshelves for the scrapbooks, but did she want them stored in a place where she could see them on a regular basis? She hesitated, then closed the flaps and set the box aside. She'd deal with that one later.

She turned back to the pile. The next one was full of her parents' wedding china, which Dad had insisted she take because he had no use for it. Hannah recalled now that there were actually *three* boxes of wedding china shoved against the wall. She couldn't bear the idea of donating the dishes, but there was zero room in her kitchen for them. Someday she and Liam would buy a house, right? And when they did, she'd have a place for her parents' china.

With a wry chuckle, she scooted the three boxes of wedding china to where the scrapbook box sat. This was going great.

Her phone rang from the kitchen, and she dashed around the piles to get to it before the call went to voicemail. The effort was worthwhile, because the caller was Liam.

"Hello, favorite fiancé," she greeted him. "How's my heroic fireman this morning?"

"Good, other than missing you," Liam said in his deep voice. "What are you up to?"

"Dealing with those boxes Dad brought me. I'm trying to make space for Aunt Fiona, but so far all I've managed to do is rearrange them."

Liam chuckled. "That's still progress."

"Not the kind of progress I need. When the sleeper sofa is out, she'll have no space to walk if I don't get rid of some things, and there are too many to just shove into my room," Hannah said, as much to remind herself as to inform him. "What's been going on with you?"

As Liam talked about his evening of helping with some intentional burns meant to contain the wildfire, Hannah pictured him looking dashing in his uniform. Liam had black hair, dark eyes, and the kindest smile she'd ever seen. What a blessing that this godly man was hers.

"But the wind shifted last night," Liam continued, "so we're being sent to a different location than they'd originally planned today."

"What level of worried do I need to be?" Hannah asked as she drew another box toward her for inspection.

"Today Archer and I are helping to get a town evacuated, so not very. My day will just be a lot of hard conversations trying to convince people they really do need to leave. There are always a few stubborn ones."

"I believe in your abilities. You can be very persuasive when you need to be."

In the background, Hannah could hear male voices. Then Liam said, "I need to go, but I'll try to call you tonight. I love you."

"Love you too," Hannah said.

She set her phone aside and opened the flaps of a new box. This one was full of tablecloths, a shower curtain, and other linens that she no longer needed but could be useful to someone else. With a sigh of relief, Hannah moved her first box into a "donation" pile.

Buoyed by the sound of Liam's voice and one box successfully allocated to the church garage sale, Hannah opened the flaps of the next box. This one was full of purses, scarves, and high heels that she hadn't touched or even thought about since her days of living in Los Angeles. She pushed a second box into the garage sale pile.

The stack diminished until the only boxes remaining were the scrapbooks, the china, and a box brimming with childhood nostalgia: a dress Hannah made with her grandmother in elementary school, the stuffed cat she had taken everywhere as a kid, and other similar items that nobody else would want. Then she scoured her apartment for nooks and crannies to tuck extra items into, and with extreme domestic creativity found places for everything either under her bed, up on the highest shelves of closets, or in the hard-to-reach recesses of cabinets.

By lunchtime, Hannah had carried her donations down to her Subaru Outback, and the boxes had all been vanquished from her apartment. She stood in the living room, beaming at the cleared space, and marveled that her apartment felt so much bigger with the stacks out of the way. Though her eye couldn't help catching on the dust and crumbling brick mortar that the boxes had been hiding.

She traipsed downstairs to the Hot Spot's supply closet and had just returned to her apartment with a broom and several microfiber cloths when her phone chirped.

The text was from Aunt Fiona. I've been thinking about sleeping arrangements. I'm typically up before the sun and in bed at nine. Not so sure that works with the hours you keep at the restaurant.

Hannah grimaced. She hadn't thought about that. When was the last time she had been in bed before eleven, much less nine? The Hot Spot didn't even close until ten p.m., and the soundproofing between the restaurant and apartment wasn't very good. Typically, there was no need for it to be because if the restaurant was open, Hannah was there. She doubted her aunt would be able to fall asleep up here with all the restaurant noise.

Maybe it would be better for Aunt Fiona to stay with Dad and Uncle Gordon. She hoped her aunt wouldn't take that suggestion as a sign that Hannah wasn't enthusiastic about the upcoming visit, because she absolutely was.

She was in the middle of drafting a response when Aunt Fiona texted again. TALKED TO YOUR DAD, AND HE AGREED IT'D BE BETTER FOR ME TO STAY IN HIS GUEST ROOM. IS THAT OKAY WITH YOU?

Well, that made things easier. Hannah erased everything she'd typed and started again. YES. WOULD'VE LOVED TO HAVE YOU AT MY PLACE, BUT I THINK YOU'RE RIGHT. CAN'T WAIT TO SEE YOU ON FRIDAY!

Hannah set her phone on the coffee table. She was still glad to have the work done, even if Aunt Fiona wasn't going to stay with her. With the baby shower on Sunday, it would be nice to have the boxes gone. She might as well finish clearing everything out, and then she'd reward herself with a lunch break.

She used the broom to sweep away a cobweb near the ceiling and then ran the bristles along the corner, where the exposed brick of the exterior met drywall. She winced when even more mortar crumbled free around a brick. How bad did the wall have to be before she needed to hire somebody to help with a repair? Hopefully

Dad, a retired electrician, or Uncle Gordon, a retired plumber, knew somebody who could take on a tiny masonry job. Or maybe it was a small enough job that the two of them could do it. Was it just the mortar that was loose, or the brick too?

Hannah grabbed the brick and groaned when half of it came free with little resistance. She didn't know much about these matters, but it didn't seem like a good sign that she could just pull a brick free. She tilted her head to peer into the space behind the brick, praying she didn't see any natural light coming through.

There wasn't any natural light, but there was *something.*

She set the half-brick on the ground and reached into the cavity. Her fingers closed around paper and something smooth and plastic. Heart racing, she retrieved the items from the hole. She turned the plastic octagon over in her fingers and ran her thumb over the dusty face of a compass. Hannah couldn't explain why the item made her smile, but it did. She'd never used a compass before, and an odd thrill went through her as she spun slowly and watched the needle adjust.

The paper she had withdrawn was lined notebook paper, yellowed with age and folded multiple times. With careful fingers, Hannah unfolded the paper. The handwriting was distinctly feminine, a loopy cursive with embellishments like tiny circles instead of dots for periods.

June 7th, 1986

Dear Apollo,

The concession stand at the pool is so boring. It's enough to make me wish school was still in session. No, not really. How's your summer going?

And of course I would never believe that about your mom! I can't believe you'd think otherwise. Your mom would never, ever do anything like that, and I will defend her to anyone I hear saying those horrible things.

I promise to check in on her while you're on your camping trip.

Write back soon! I'm so bored!

Sunflower

Hannah read the note twice and then turned the page over in her hand. Dust floated off the paper and tickled her nose, but there wasn't any more writing on the back.

Who were Apollo and Sunflower? And how did this letter and compass end up tucked away—perhaps *hidden* away—behind a brick in what used to be the old firehouse?

Chapter Three

"No." Lacy dragged out the syllable. "I'm very sure that I would remember if I met somebody named Apollo or Sunflower."

Hannah rolled a fork and spoon—or "pitchfork" and "shovel" as they'd be labeled at the baby shower—in a red gingham napkin, and set it in the basket with the others. "They must be nicknames, right?"

"Not necessarily." Lacy flipped the note over to investigate the back. "I've spent a lot of time on baby name websites recently, and there are loads of unusual names out there."

"Speaking of which, are you and Neil any closer to picking a name?"

Hannah knew that Lacy and Neil didn't plan to share their names until the baby was born, and she respected that decision. But she would love to sit around and toss out baby name ideas with her best friend.

Lacy's mouth pursed. "Not really. Neil, of course, wants to name our child something epic like Shakespeare or Copernicus—"

Hannah couldn't keep a snort of laughter from escaping.

"—but I can't picture looking at my newborn baby's face and saying, 'Good morning, Copernicus.'" Lacy smoothed her lightweight summer blouse over her increasingly round belly. "I'm sure we'll figure it out."

Hannah quelled her amused smile. "Of course you will."

"It just feels like such a huge responsibility," Lacy said. "I mean, I name farm animals all the time, but naming an actual human feels different."

Now Hannah allowed her amused smile to come forth. "Speaking of responsibility, did you know that even after you name the baby, you also have to raise it?"

Lacy giggled. "What?" she asked with mock surprise. "It's starting to sound like my whole life is about to change when this baby arrives."

Hannah laughed too. While it was cliché to say that a pregnant woman "glowed," that was the exact word she thought when she saw Lacy these days. Yes, her friend often looked uncomfortable, but she radiated happiness.

Hannah glanced at the timer on her electric pressure cooker where she was preparing the eggs for the "baby chick" deviled eggs for Sunday's shower. Even though it was only Thursday, she had made herself a list of all the preparatory things that she could get ready early for the baby shower, like boiling the eggs, making piecrust for the mini quiches, and washing the mason jars they'd use for glasses.

Theoretically there was still plenty of time to prepare for the party, but tomorrow, Hannah had promised to help her dad get the guest room ready for Aunt Fiona, and she wanted to be available to spend time with her aunt on Saturday. She set aside the finished silverware rolls and started on the piecrust.

Hannah hadn't anticipated Lacy stopping by her apartment this morning while she was in the midst of shower preparations, but she was always glad to see her best friend. Before too long, Lacy would be lugging around a car seat and a diaper bag when she stopped by. Assuming she would still do things like "stop by" after the baby was born.

Hannah frowned. Of course Lacy would still stop by. Maybe not as often, and she would have a baby's sleeping and feeding schedule to work around, on top of all her usual work on the farm. But they would still have times like this.

Wouldn't they?

"I don't know." Lacy laid Sunflower's note on the kitchen counter. "This sure sounds like a note passed between teenagers, but how did it end up here at the fire station? It doesn't make sense to me."

Hannah pushed away her doubts about what their friendship would look like in a few months and considered the question. "Maybe Apollo was a fireman? Or had an older brother who was?"

Lacy raised her eyebrows. "And he thought, 'I'll just stick my compass and note behind this brick?' Why?"

"We're throwing out ideas, right?" Hannah said as she scooped flour. "They don't have to be *good* ideas."

Lacy grinned. "Okay, fair." She rose from the barstool and considered Hannah's living space. "Was that corner originally in one of the sleeping rooms?"

Hannah pulled up the mental image of her apartment before they'd knocked down walls. "No, it was a common area. A living room of sorts."

Lacy continued to stare at the wall. "I don't get it. Why hide something private in a semipublic space?"

"Maybe home wasn't safe," Hannah suggested. "*Something* was going on, right? Sunflower talks about Apollo's mom and rumors going around. Maybe Apollo couldn't keep this note or his compass at home anymore. Though I'm not sure what would be so private about a compass."

"I wonder if I could find them in a yearbook." Lacy angled the note toward the kitchen lights. "It would have been 1986. I need to stop by the library anyway. I'll peek at a yearbook while I'm there. Maybe I'll even find good baby names during the search."

Hannah chuckled. "Sunflower seems like a great choice if you have a girl. She'd be born in August, and her mama is a farmer. I think it's worth considering."

"Sunflower certainly wouldn't be my *last* choice," Lacy replied. "Topic change. Have you heard from Liam since he left?"

"Yes." Hannah reached for the salt canister. "He's very busy there, of course, but we've talked every day so far."

"When does he get back?"

Hannah sighed. "I don't know, and neither does he. Liam was hoping that if he and Archer were in Wyoming for a week, they could help the community get through the worst of the fire, but I guess the region has high winds right now, and that's really causing some problems."

"High winds sound like the opposite of what they need."

"It is." Hannah leveled the teaspoon of salt and added it to the dough mixture. "I just want him to be home in time to meet Aunt Fiona."

"How long is she staying?"

"I'm not sure about that either, but she sent me a text this morning saying she might be here through the end of the month, if we don't mind. She finished her contract at the hospital in DC, so she doesn't need to get back for work. As I understand it, she'll be waiting for a new placement while she's here."

"How often does she move?" Lacy asked.

"About every six months, unless she wants to stay longer."

"Wow. As somebody who has been tied to a piece of land her whole life, I can't even imagine being that nomadic."

"It's definitely a different lifestyle," Hannah said as she pulled butter from the refrigerator. "I think she loves it, though."

"I'm excited to meet her." Lacy looked at her phone screen. "I guess I should get going. Everything takes me longer than it used to, and I told Neil I'd bring him lunch."

Hannah wiped her floury hands on her apron. "I'm glad you stopped by."

"Me too. Who knows how much longer I'll be able to drop in on you like this?" Lacy smiled, but it didn't quite reach her eyes.

Hannah forced a brightness into her voice that she didn't feel. "I know it'll be more challenging once the baby arrives, but we'll figure it out."

Lacy chuckled. "I wasn't even thinking about that. I was thinking about Liam. That once you're married, you might not be as receptive to me popping over for a chat."

Hannah hadn't considered how *her* life would be changing. She'd only thought of Lacy's. "Of course I'll still want you to come by."

Lacy kept her eyes trained on her purse as she slung it over her shoulder. "You say that now, but—"

"I'll say it as Mrs. Berthold too." Hannah's voice was firm. "You will always be welcome at my house. *Always.*"

Lacy's smile wasn't as full as usual, but it didn't look as strained as before. "Okay. There's just a lot of change on the horizon. You and Liam, me and the baby..."

Hannah came around the counter and wrapped her arms around her friend. "I know, but *this* won't change."

Though even as she said the words—even as she longed for the sentiment to be true—she suspected this was a promise she couldn't keep. Her upcoming marriage, and Lacy being a mother, would change their lives in ways that neither of them could anticipate. As much as Hannah wanted their friendship to look exactly like it did at this moment, she knew that was unlikely in light of all the other changes.

Change was coming, whether she wanted it to or not.

"You wouldn't think something like having the parking lot repaved would make such a big difference, but it really does," Raquel was saying to Elaine as Hannah breezed through the dining room.

The restaurant was less crowded than on a typical Friday. Raquel stood beside Elaine at the hostess stand, using the odd lull in activity for a conversation while they still could. Seeing two of her employees connect like this made Hannah's chest swell with pride.

"I used to have to drive so slowly through the parking lot because there were all these potholes, and now it feels like I'm gliding into my spot," Raquel continued.

Elaine nodded along. "The right management company makes a huge difference. I'm so glad yours changed, because I know you've had problems."

"Oddly, it's still managed by Lawrence Underhill Properties, but according to an email we got last month, Lawrence retired and his daughter took over." Raquel smiled. "The location is great, and the building is so beautiful and historic, which is why I wanted to live there in the first place. I'm excited that management is showing signs of taking care of the place and its residents."

"That's good news for the whole community. We need our historic buildings to be cared for. Oh, here we go," Elaine said as a group of young moms who ate at the Hot Spot every week approached the door. "Happy Friday, ladies. Raquel will show you to your usual table."

Hannah welcomed each of the women by name as Raquel led them to their booth, then she turned to Elaine. "I'm heading to my dad's place because my aunt is about to arrive. I'm going to have dinner with them, but I should be back by seven thirty. If Jacob gets too slammed in the kitchen, I'm only a phone call away."

Elaine dismissed her with a wave. "We've got this, boss. Have a good time."

Hannah knew her team could handle everything just fine, and she'd done a lot of prep work in the kitchen to ease the potential strain of her being gone tonight, but she still struggled with the idea of being away from the Hot Spot on a traditionally busy night. Or any time they were open, really.

Hannah headed into the humid afternoon heat. She could practically feel her hair frizzing on the short walk to her car.

When she arrived at her dad's, Hannah immediately heard his border terrier, Zeus, announcing her presence. She spotted him in a front window, his paws pressed to the glass and his thick stump of a tail wagging with delight.

Hannah opened the front door and called, "Hello?" as she rubbed Zeus behind the ears.

"I'm in the laundry room!" came Dad's muffled reply.

Zeus trotted along behind Hannah as she traveled the hallway to find her dad crouched in front of the dryer, pulling fresh sheets from within. "Hi, Dad."

"Hi, pumpkin." His knees popped as he stood. "Our guest sheets smelled dusty, so I thought I'd give them a wash."

"I'm sure Aunt Fiona will appreciate that. How are things going?"

"Great. Everything is done after I get these on the bed. If you want to start on dinner, I'll be in to help in a minute."

"Sounds good."

Hannah headed to the kitchen with Zeus trotting along behind her. Soon, Dad joined her.

"I had to ask around at the store about jicama," he said when he saw Hannah dicing the round root vegetable.

Hannah grinned. "I predict that after you eat my pineapple jicama salsa on a fish taco, this won't be the last jicama you buy."

"I love everything you cook," her dad said, tying on an apron. "It's just the three of us tonight, by the way. Gordon is watching the kids so Maeve and Hunter can go out."

"Oh, how nice," Hannah said. Maeve was Uncle Gordon's daughter.

"I've been thinking about what to do with Fiona while she's in town. There's a place to rent paddleboards at Lake Blackberry now. That seems like something she'd like. Or she might enjoy Mammoth Cave. I don't know how long it's been since she was there. If she wants to do that, we'll need to see if we can reserve a tour."

Hannah pulled open her dad's refrigerator and reveled in the cool air that flowed out. "There's a new restaurant in Glasgow that I've wanted to try, assuming she likes Thai food. Want me to grab the fish fillets?"

"Please."

Hannah handed the package to her dad and then pulled the remaining ingredients she needed from the refrigerator. As he seasoned the fish for the grill, he told her about the mystery novel he was reading, complete with a list of potential suspects and who he thought was most likely to have committed the crime. Hannah grinned to hear him speaking about the characters as though they were real people he knew.

"Speaking of mysteries," she said as she scraped the diced pineapple into a pretty bowl with the other ingredients. "When I was cleaning a few days ago, I found the oddest thing behind a brick in my wall—a compass and an old note, written in 1986."

"Really?" Dad leaned forward on his elbows, clearly intrigued. "Who wrote the note?"

"I don't know. It was signed 'Sunflower' and addressed to 'Apollo.' Do you know anyone in town with those names?"

"Sunflower and Apollo? Definitely not. I would remember those."

Hannah stirred lime juice into the fresh salsa and scooted the bowl aside. "I'm guessing they were teenagers. Or at least Sunflower was."

Dad shook his head. "I wish I could help, but it was well after my time. The grill pan is in the drawer underneath the oven."

Hannah crouched to pull out the requested appliance. "Lacy and I don't recognize the names at all, nor can we figure out why the note and compass would've been left in the fire station."

"Good questions," Dad said, the words garbled as if his mouth was full.

Hannah peeked over the countertop to find her father sampling the fresh salsa.

He grinned at her as he lifted a chip covered in salsa to his mouth. "I'm hungry."

She laughed and turned on the heat for searing the fish. "Just leave some for Aunt Fiona."

"No promises." Dad reached for another chip. "Are you sure the note was written by a teenager?"

"Fairly sure. The handwriting looks like a teenage girl's, and she references working at the pool and wishing she was back in school."

Dad swallowed. "Certainly does sound like a teenager. Maybe she volunteered at the firehouse?"

"Maybe." Hannah searched through the cooking utensils, hunting for tongs she liked and not finding any that were ideal. She should get him some for his birthday in October. Good tongs made all the difference. "Whoever Sunflower was, she was reassuring Apollo that she didn't believe the rumors about his mom. Do you remember any scandals or rumors from around then?"

"In 1986, the majority of my brainpower was in use convincing your mom to marry me. An asteroid could've crashed in Blackberry Valley and I wouldn't have noticed."

Hannah giggled. From what she remembered of stories about her parents, it didn't take Dad much "convincing" to get Mom to marry him. While her dad was no longer the man in the wedding photos—trim build and dark hair—Hannah thought he was even more handsome now. Her parents had been deeply devoted to each other, and because of their example, Hannah had known that it was worth it for her to be patient and wait for someone like Liam Berthold. The kind of man who would take time away from work to go help firefighters in a different community.

"Honey, I can grill the fish," Dad said as Hannah laid a fish filet across the grill pan. "You relax."

She handed Dad the tongs. "Sounds good to me."

He had just finished getting the fish on the grill when Zeus launched into a string of barks and ran for the front door. Hannah glanced at the glowing numbers on the microwave—nearly six thirty. Aunt Fiona must have arrived. As she followed her dad to the door, her heart squeezed in excitement. Despite Liam being gone right now, she was really looking forward to the next few weeks.

Chapter Four

When Hannah saw Aunt Fiona step out of her small, sporty car, her breath caught. Aunt Fiona looked much more like Hannah's mom than Hannah had remembered. Aunt Fiona wore her age well. Her silvery blond hair was long enough to be pulled back in a ponytail, and the glasses she wore were stylish without looking too young for her. She wore a loose-fitting skirt that hit below her knees and a sleeveless white shirt that showed her toned arms. Hannah thought it was possible—likely, even—that her aunt could do more push-ups than she could.

Aunt Fiona squealed, and her green eyes crinkled at the corners. "My darling niece. Get over here!"

Hannah jogged the last few steps to her aunt and wrapped her in a big hug. She hadn't realized how deeply she missed her until just now.

"Look at you." Aunt Fiona cupped Hannah's face and beamed with the indulgent love of an aunt. "You resemble Frieda so strongly."

"I was thinking the same thing about you," Hannah said, her voice watery. Tears built in her eyes.

Aunt Fiona's smile wavered. They held each other's gaze for a moment, and then Hannah's aunt released her and turned to Dad. "Hello, Gabriel. It's been ages."

"Far too long." Dad stepped in to hug Aunt Fiona. "How are you?"

"Happy to be home. Thanks for taking me in."

"Of course. Hannah's fixed up a feast for us."

"All I did was the salsa. Dad's doing everything else." With a jolt, Hannah remembered the fish on the grill pan inside and rushed for the door. "Dad, the fish!"

Dad laughed as he lifted one of Aunt Fiona's suitcases from the trunk of the car. "It'll be fine. We'll just have *blackened* fish tacos."

The fish was only slightly blackened, and the salsa did a good job of hiding any dryness that might've been there. Hannah tried to ignore the clock. She knew she needed to get back to the restaurant, but it was hard to leave Aunt Fiona's bubbly, warm presence.

"I want to hear all the details of your wedding plans." Aunt Fiona set her half-eaten taco on her plate and fixed Hannah with her gaze, as if wedding plans required all her attention. "I cannot wait to meet this handsome fireman of yours. Did you know that Lori Berthold went to our church when I was growing up? Of course she wasn't Lori *Berthold* at the time. I can't think of what her maiden name was now."

"Meyer," Hannah supplied with a smile. Liam's parents, Lori and Daniel, lived in Florida now. Hannah had met them a few months ago, and they were both lovely people. Which was no surprise, considering the man Liam was.

"Yes, Lori Meyer! Anyway. I thought she was the absolute coolest. She had this gorgeous long hair—black and thick and lovely. She usually wore it in a French braid."

"Liam has black hair," Hannah said.

"I remember when Lori was pregnant with him. She was the cutest pregnant woman you've ever seen, like she'd swallowed a basketball. And now to think that baby is going to be my..." Aunt Fiona frowned. "What will Liam's and my relationship be? Do we say nephew-in-law? Is that a thing?"

Dad nodded. "It definitely is."

Aunt Fiona picked up her taco once more. "Regardless of what the relation is technically called, he'll be family. I can't wait to meet him. The grown-up version of him, I mean."

"You'll love him," Hannah said. "I wish he was in town, but right now he's in Wyoming helping to control the wildfires up there."

"Is he?" Aunt Fiona made a show of fanning her face. "What a hero. I was just reading about those this morning. They had to evacuate a hospital yesterday. I can't even imagine what a chore *that* is. You must be so proud of him."

Hannah beamed. "Extremely."

"Does he know when he can come home, or does it depend on the fire?"

"Depends on the fire. Unfortunately, the weather hasn't been very cooperative." Hannah glanced at her watch and pushed the last of her taco into her mouth. "I'm so sorry, but I have to get back to the restaurant. Friday is always a busy night for us and—"

"No need to apologize." Aunt Fiona stood to give Hannah another hug. "We will have plenty of time to catch up these next couple of weeks. I'm so excited to experience this restaurant of yours."

"It's really something, Fiona." Dad looked at Hannah, his eyes gleaming with pride. "We'll go for dinner while you're here."

Aunt Fiona clapped her hands together with enthusiasm. "Wonderful idea."

Hannah took in both of their expressions and felt deeply loved. What a gift they were to her. "I'll save the best table for you."

"Maybe Drew and his family could meet us there," Aunt Fiona suggested as she trailed Hannah to the door. "AJ was a baby the last time I saw them, and I've never met their other two."

"You're in for a treat," Dad said. "You've never met such wonderful kids."

"Agreed. Not that we're biased or anything." Hannah grinned and then hugged them both at the door. "See you tomorrow."

Hannah was in the middle of carrying another load of groceries up to her apartment—nobody would go hungry at tomorrow's baby shower—when she felt her phone buzz in her back pocket. She set down the bags on the stairs and fumbled for her phone.

"I'm not in labor," Lacy greeted her. "That's what Neil thinks every time I call him these days."

Hannah chuckled. "A side effect of being pregnant, I suppose."

"Where are you? It sounds echoey."

"The stairwell on my way up to my apartment. How are you? Other than not being in labor, that is."

"Fine, although my ankles are enormous. I'm lying on the couch with my feet elevated to try to get the swelling down, and the Blackberry Valley High School yearbook of 1986 is keeping me company."

Hannah hooked her arm through her bags once more and continued her climb upstairs. "Really? Evangeline let you bring it home?"

"No, but after the library I was dropping off eggs for Suzanne Lake. I knew she graduated in '89, so I thought she might have the 1986 yearbook. She did."

Hannah bumped her hip against her apartment door to open it. While she knew that Suzanne Lake ran a cookie-decorating business out of her home, she didn't know much else. "You just happened to know that Suzanne was in the class of 1989?"

Lacy laughed. "It came up a couple weeks ago during a delivery. She made a comment that she graduated high school the year before I was born. Now, why my brain filed away *that* information but I can't remember where I put my sunglasses, I have no idea."

Hannah giggled. "Me neither, but that sounds familiar. Have you learned anything interesting from the yearbook?"

"All I've learned is that Sunflower and Apollo are not in here. Not listed with those names, anyway."

Hannah's hope deflated. "I guess that's not a surprise. We thought they might be nicknames, after all."

"I should've asked Suzanne if she knew who they were. I asked Evangeline when I was at the library, and she clearly assumed that Neil and I are dedicated to the idea of a unique name for our child. She said she's never known an Apollo or a Sunflower in Blackberry Valley, and that she thought they sounded like lovely choices for our baby."

Hannah couldn't withhold her laughter. "Apollo Shakespeare Minyard. It's perfect."

"Or, if we have a girl, Sunflower Desdemona Minyard," Lacy said through her own giggles.

"Desdemona?" Hannah echoed. "Is that on the list?"

"Not on mine. But if it's a name longer than eight letters and tied to literature at all, it's on Neil's name list. I think that's what he's doing all day long at Legend & Key—flipping through books for cumbersome names from literature to bestow upon our child."

Hannah set the bags of groceries on her kitchen counter. "I asked both Dad and Liam, and neither of them know any Apollos or Sunflowers either."

"Bummer. That was a good idea, though. Between the two of them, I think they know the whole town."

"And Liam confirmed that the corner where I found the letter and compass was formerly in the common area. He said when he's back in town, he can look through records to see who was employed in 1986 and therefore would've been spending time in the firehouse. I told him that I don't know if he needs to go to the trouble. Obviously the note wasn't written by a fireman."

"True, but it could still be helpful information," Lacy said. "Whoever they were, they must've had a connection to the fire-house, right? Maybe it was Sunflower or Apollo's father. Maybe they visited him at work. If we know who worked at the station in 1986, we can find out who had teenage kids."

This was a good point. Hannah would love to return the compass and the note to the original owner, but her own to-do list was crowding out her capacity to devote much time to the project. There was a baby shower to host, an aunt to enjoy, a wedding to plan, and a restaurant to run.

On the other end of the call, Lacy made a grunting noise.

Hannah's heart rate spiked. "Are you in labor *now*?"

"No," Lacy said with a laugh. "Just shifting positions on the couch. It takes some work these days." She made another noise and then sighed. "There we go. Much better. Just a few more weeks of this. Oh, you know who I *did* see in the yearbook? Rusty Studebaker. The bookkeeper extraordinaire was a freshman in 1986 and had a spectacular mullet. Neil's going to give him grief for it the next time they talk."

Hannah tried to picture Rusty—with his polo shirt and close-cropped haircut—sporting a mullet. "I went through that bangs phase in high school, so I guess I shouldn't judge too harshly."

Lacy giggled. "I'd forgotten about your bangs."

Hannah began unloading food from the shopping bags. "If Rusty was in high school in 1986, I wonder if he knows anyone who might've gone by Sunflower or Apollo?"

"Ooh, maybe," Lacy said. "Want me to have Neil ask him?"

"No, I can do it. I have a question for him about categorizing expenses anyway." Hannah chuckled. "That won't be weird at all, right? 'Here's my accounting question, and by the way, do the names Sunflower or Apollo ring any bells?'"

"Let me know what he says," Lacy said through what sounded like an epic yawn. "I think it's time for my nap. Growing a person is exhausting."

Hannah grinned as she noticed it was ten a.m. Of course, caring for a farm meant Lacy was up and working earlier than the average person. "Sounds like a good idea. Oh, real quick, how are the cottage renovations going? Do you need my help with painting or anything?"

Lacy and Neil had been working for months to get the cottage on the farm ready for her mom to move in so Christine could help with the baby.

"That's so kind of you, but Mom is doing that part herself. She'll probably move in sometime in the next couple weeks."

"I'm so glad the timing is working out," Hannah said. "It'll be wonderful to have her right there to help you."

"I know," Lacy said through another yawn. "She's the best."

"I'll let you go now. Enjoy your nap."

After Hannah hung up, she gazed at the ingredients scattered across her countertops, which would turn into tomorrow's baby shower feast. There was no way this would all fit in her refrigerator, so it was a good thing that she had a commercial refrigerator downstairs that she could use. A useful perk of owning a restaurant.

While she was thinking about it, Hannah tapped out a quick text to Rusty. Sorry this is so random, but any chance you know a couple of people from high school named Sunflower and Apollo? I found something in my apartment that I think belonged to one of them, but I'm having trouble figuring out who they are. I think they'd be about the same age as you.

A few minutes later, as Hannah fried bacon for the baby quiches, her phone vibrated with Rusty's response. Can't say that I do. What'd they leave behind?

Hannah adjusted the bacon slices so they weren't crowding one another and then typed, A compass. It's been here a while by the looks of it. Just thought they might want it back.

Maybe she should've agreed to Lacy's offer of having Neil ask Rusty about this, because Hannah felt a little silly. She put her phone away and turned her attention to mincing green onions.

A few minutes later, Rusty sent a new message. Does the compass look like this?

Hannah blinked in disbelief. Below Rusty's question was a picture of a compass identical to the one she had found in her wall. She gaped for a moment. Yes, it looks exactly like that.

A few seconds later, her screen lit with an incoming call from Rusty.

"Hi," Hannah greeted him. "I can't believe you have the same compass."

Rusty chuckled. "It's not as odd as you might think. You say this was in your apartment?"

"That's right." She cradled her phone between her shoulder and ear so she could continue dicing. "Behind a loose brick, along with a note to someone named—or nicknamed—Apollo, from Sunflower."

"That's really interesting. I have no idea why they would be there, and I've never heard those names before, but I'm fairly certain that whoever it belonged to was a Wayfinder."

"A Wayfinder?" Hannah echoed. "What's that?"

"When I was in high school, there was a man named Kenneth Cutuli who worked as a firefighter. He seemed old at the time, but he was probably younger than I am now. I think he was probably in his late forties. Anyway, he mentored a group of us boys. He taught us outdoor skills similar to what one might learn in Boy Scouts. Every boy who was in Wayfinders was given a compass like the one in the picture I sent you. I keep mine on my desk still. That's how special Wayfinders was to me."

Hannah pulled the pan of bacon off to the side so she could focus on the conversation. "How many boys were in Wayfinders?"

"It varied over the years. Sometimes there were just four or five of us. Other times nine or ten."

"What about in 1986?"

"Oh, I don't know. In 1986, I was a freshman in high school, I think. The group was bigger then. Both Lake brothers, Steve Hines,

Theo Drakos, Wilson Hartfield, and maybe another couple guys in there too. I'll have to think about it."

Hannah scribbled all the names on the back of her grocery receipt. The only two she recognized were the Lake brothers, whom she knew from around town. Edward worked for the city, and she'd had some dealings with him while opening the Hot Spot. He ate at the restaurant occasionally, but Hannah got the feeling he would prefer a more sophisticated menu. Maybe she just assumed that because every time she saw Edward, he was wearing a nice suit and tie, even during the summer.

Lincoln Lake was married to Suzanne, the woman Lacy had borrowed the yearbook from. He was younger than Edward by a couple years, and Hannah was pretty sure he did something with real estate. He often had meetings at the Hot Spot, and they usually involved his laptop displaying graphs and photographs of buildings. And he liked extra jalapeños on everything he ordered.

She tapped the names on the list, as if doing so might reveal why one of them would go by Apollo. "Does Apollo seem like a nickname any of them would've used?"

"I don't think so," Rusty said, the words slow and unsure. "That was the name on the note?"

"Yes." Hannah reached for the note. "Written on June seventh in 1986. Sounds like Sunflower worked at the pool concession stand. The only other clue is that she tells Apollo that she would of course never believe the rumors about his mother, that she knows his mom 'would never do anything like that' but that's as specific as she gets. Does that sound familiar at all?"

"Well." Rusty dragged out the word. "The first person that comes to mind is Mrs. Lake, Edward and Lincoln's mother."

Hannah frowned. "You think Sunflower is Mrs. Lake?"

"No, I'm wondering if she's the mom being referred to in the note." Rusty hesitated. "How familiar are you with the Lake family?"

"Hardly at all. I know who Edward is, of course, and Lincoln is at the Hot Spot once a week or so, but most of my conversations with them are about the weather or food."

"I figured the Lake family history might be stretching back a bit far for you. Edward and Lincoln are the only siblings who still live around here, but they're the youngest of eight kids. They had six older sisters."

Hannah couldn't resist the gasp that came out of her. She'd always felt in awe of women who raised large families. The single task of feeding that many children three meals a day seemed monumental in and of itself.

"I know," Rusty said, a smile in his voice. "Pamela and I have four kids, and our house always felt like a circus. I can't even imagine what eight would've been like. Anyway, Edward was two grades ahead of me, and Lincoln is my age. During high school, there was this big scandal—for lack of a better word—around Mrs. Lake. The school had a fundraiser so the pool could be repaired. She served as the PTA treasurer, and she supposedly stole money from the proceeds."

Hannah winced. Having lived in Blackberry Valley for much of her life, she could imagine how pervasive the gossip would've been over a situation like that. "Oh, dear."

"I honestly don't know how the situation resolved. We were teenage boys, and I felt strange about the idea of reaching out to

Lincoln or Edward to ask how they were doing, or if they needed anything. Kenneth probably did, but not in front of all the Wayfinders, of course."

Hannah wasn't surprised that Rusty had never talked to the Lake brothers about such a tender situation. In high school, she and Lacy had shared every concern or thought that popped into their heads. But when her younger brother, Drew, hung out with his friends, the talk was all about video games and sports, no matter what hardships they might have been going through in real life.

"Hopefully Kenneth talked to them," Hannah said. "Even if Mrs. Lake didn't actually steal from the fundraiser and those were just rumors, that alone in a town the size of Blackberry Valley would be hard to deal with."

"Lincoln probably talked to his girlfriend about it, because I remember hearing more from Suzanne than anybody else. She was adamant that Mrs. Lake didn't steal that money." Rusty paused. "I guess *she* could be Sunflower. She had blond hair, so maybe that was a nickname of some kind? And Apollo wouldn't be a stretch for Lincoln, I suppose. Isn't Apollo supposed to be attractive?"

Hannah wrote *Apollo?* next to Lincoln's name. "Maybe? My recollection of Greek mythology isn't very good."

"Neither is mine. All I know is that Lincoln never had a shortage of girls hanging around, even though he and Suzanne were always an item. I think they're still married."

"As far as I know."

"Edward always did okay with girls too, but I never heard anyone call either of them Apollo."

Hannah tapped her pencil on the counter as she thought. "Any idea why their compass and a note about their mother would've ended up hidden in the firehouse?"

"Afraid not," Rusty said. "I mean, Kenneth worked there, but none of us ever hung out at the station. All our meetings were at his house. I can't think of any reason why that compass or note would've been hidden at the station."

That was disappointing. Hannah didn't have any ideas either. "I guess it'll have to remain a mystery."

"Yeah," Rusty said. "For *now.* I've heard about you, Hannah Prentiss. Mysteries don't stay mysteries very long once they've caught your attention."

Chapter Five

Exclamations of, "Isn't that the cutest thing?" and "I wish those existed back when *I* had babies!" filled Hannah's apartment with each gift Lacy opened. To Lacy's left, Lorelai Dawson, the pastor's wife, made notes about each present so Lacy could write thank-you notes later, and to Lacy's right sat Connie Sanchez, the church secretary, ready to take discarded wrapping paper. When everyone was done oohing and aahing over a specific item, Lacy's mom, Christine, would whisk away the opened present and hand her daughter a new one.

Since Lacy was being adequately hovered over, Hannah split her time between watching her open gifts, keeping an eye on the dwindling food supplies, and chatting with Bryn Reynolds, whose fiancé, Archer, was in Wyoming with Liam.

"I'm not even sure what half these things are," Bryn confessed to Hannah.

Hannah watched as Lacy set aside something that was maybe a drying rack for bottles. Maybe. "Yeah, that one was a mystery."

"I'm clueless about babies. Absolutely clueless. Archer wants a whole litter of kids, but I think we should start with one and see what we think."

"Seems sensible to me."

"How many kids do you and Liam want? Sorry. Is that too personal? My mom says that sometimes I ask questions that are too personal."

Hannah grinned. "No, it's fine. We're not sure. More than one, but probably no more than three."

"If we have more than one, I want either two or four. Otherwise somebody gets left out."

Hannah could see that point. She thought of her nephews outnumbering her niece, or how sometimes the older two made the youngest feel left out. But of course, she and Drew had had their share of arguments as kids too. "I think that's just how siblings are."

"You're probably right." Bryn gnawed at her thumbnail, looking as anxious as if she really did have to decide right now how many children she'd have. "Maybe just one, then."

Elaine touched Hannah's elbow, drawing her attention. "Do you still want the chafing dishes on?"

"Probably not. Thanks for the reminder." Hannah excused herself from Bryn and followed Elaine to the long counter where all the food was arranged. "Let's leave desserts where they are, but I think everything else can be put away."

"I'm happy to take care of that so you can watch Lacy open gifts."

"That's so kind of you, but you should get to watch too. We'll do it together, and then it'll go fast." Hannah glanced at Lacy, who was holding up a package of diapers. The package struck her as overly fancy, considering what diapers were used for. "And I can see fine from here, anyway."

In the not-too-distant future, it might be her sitting in Lacy's seat, holding up onesies and expensive diapers while women talked in nostalgic voices about their own babies. Hannah had always liked kids, always imagined she would have them "someday," but it was unsettling to realize that "someday" was drawing closer. Within a couple years, her life might look very different than it did right now. The thought wasn't exactly unwelcome, but the idea of so much change at once made her stomach twist uncomfortably.

Hannah turned her focus to putting away food, something she did regularly, and felt her body relax with the familiar rhythm. There wasn't much left over, thankfully, and she and Elaine made quick work of putting away what needed to be refrigerated and rearranging the desserts to be more prominent for anyone who wanted more.

Fifteen minutes later, Lacy finished opening her gifts, and Lorelai had them all gather around to say a prayer over the Minyard family. When she finished, Hannah didn't see a single dry eye among the guests and passed around a box of tissues. The women gathered their purses, gave Lacy hugs, and grabbed one more brownie or cookie for the road. Based on the smile Lacy wore, Hannah decided the baby shower had been a complete success.

"What a lovely group of women," Christine said as she, Hannah, and Connie carried the last of the gifts out to Lacy's truck.

"Everyone was so generous," Lacy said. "I think this cleaned out our gift registry."

"Good thing too," Connie said. "You don't have much longer."

"I know." Lacy's hand trailed down her abdomen. "August felt so far away when we found out I was pregnant. I can't believe it's almost here."

For a few minutes, the four of them worked to arrange all the gifts in the cab of the truck. After Hannah wedged a final package of diapers into place, she turned to hug her best friend. "There's enough leftover food that you shouldn't have to make dinner tonight. I put the containers in the passenger seat, so hopefully your mom doesn't mind holding them in her lap."

"Not having to cook is the *real* gift," Lacy said with a laugh. She pulled back from the hug. "Before I forget, I left the 1986 yearbook in your apartment. When you're done, you can give it back to me."

"Thank you." Hannah beamed at her best friend. "I love you. I can't wait to meet this baby."

After several more hugs, Hannah and Connie stood on the sidewalk and waved goodbye to Lacy and Christine.

"Neil and Lacy are going to be such good parents," Connie said, using her hand to shield her eyes from the late afternoon sun.

"The best," Hannah agreed. "Do you have any fun plans this evening?"

"Hal and I are watching *Casablanca* tonight. Most Sunday nights, we pick a classic movie to watch together. We've done that for years."

"What a sweet tradition."

"We started it when the kids were still living at home. When you're raising children together, it's very easy to become so busy managing their lives that you forget to pay attention to each other."

Hannah had heard things like this but found it baffling. How could she ever *not* pay attention to Liam?

The question must have been clear on her face because Connie smiled. "Hard to imagine now, probably. Hal and I found that having a routine date on the calendar got us through some busy seasons and hard times. Even though the kids moved out ages ago, we still have Sunday movie nights."

Hannah smiled at the thought of Connie and Hal sitting side-by-side on the couch, watching old movies together for decades. "I love that."

Connie turned toward the door up to Hannah's apartment. "I'm going to help you clean up before I go."

"You don't have to do that."

"I know I don't, but I don't want you stuck with a messy place. Many hands make light work, as they say."

Hannah opened her mouth to protest, but Connie had already started up the stairs. Anything Hannah said—besides *thank you*—would be a waste. When it came to helping people, Connie could be extremely pushy, in the best of ways.

While Hannah cleaned the chafing dishes that belonged to the Hot Spot, Connie flitted around the room, collecting cups and plates and silverware that had been scattered about.

"You've done such a lovely job with this space," she said. "You've struck a great balance of updating it while preserving the historical integrity."

"Thank you." Hannah felt a rush of pride. "I'd never lived in an old building before, and I was a bit nervous about it, but I've really enjoyed the experience."

Connie nodded. "Older homes can be delightful. Hal and I moved into an old place that had a dumbwaiter, which I found charming. They can also be not-so-delightful too, I suppose. Neither of us loved having to replace all the old pipes in there."

"I understand that for sure. Earlier this week, I actually found something hidden in the wall."

"You did?" Connie's blue eyes widened behind her glasses. "How did something stay hidden in your wall all these years?"

"Not *in* the wall, I guess, but behind a brick." Hannah crossed the room to the corner and wiggled out the half-brick to show Connie.

Connie bent and looked inside the empty space. "You couldn't hide much in there, could you?"

"No. It was a compass and a note from 1986. You don't happen to know anybody named Sunflower or Apollo, do you?"

Connie frowned. "I don't think so. Probably nicknames, right?"

"That's what I think. I spoke with Rusty Studebaker about it yesterday. Do you know him?"

"Oh, sweet Rusty." Connie wore a wistful expression. "Yes, I do. I was friends with his older sister. How is he?"

"Good. He's doing bookkeeping work for me now, thanks to Neil's recommendation. Anyway, Rusty said the compass was one given out to a group of boys called Wayfinders. Are you familiar with them?"

Connie crouched to pick up a cup. "Can't say that I am."

"According to Rusty, it was similar to Boy Scouts, but it was led by one of the firemen, Kenneth Cutuli."

Connie nodded. "That sounds like Kenneth. He was wonderful. As was Joan, his wife. The Cutulis were the kind of people who were always looking for ways to help others or improve the community. They moved to Florida a decade ago, which is where their kids settled. I don't know if either of them are still alive. They'd probably be in their nineties, if they are."

"Rusty had all kinds of nice things to say about Kenneth and the Wayfinders group he led. It sounds like the group really had an impact on the boys. Rusty still keeps his compass on his desk."

"I'm sure it would mean a lot to Kenneth to know that. All he ever wanted in life was a chance to help others." Connie watched as Hannah fit the brick back into its slot. "I wonder why somebody left the compass behind. You said there was a note?"

"Yes. It was from Sunflower to Apollo. I agree with you that they're probably nicknames. Rusty thought that Apollo might be one of the Lake brothers, because the note said something about how she knew his mom didn't do what people were saying she did."

"I see," Connie said. "Rusty assumes they were talking about Mrs. Lake, then? About what happened with the school fundraiser?"

"Yes, though Rusty wasn't sure how that situation resolved."

Connie's mouth pressed into a line. "You said 1986? That'd be about right for the timing."

Hope fluttered in Hannah's chest. She might be closer to figuring out who these items belonged to. "So you agree the note was probably for one of the Lake brothers?"

"Well, I don't know anything about either of them being called Apollo, but it's true that Mrs. Lake stole money from the fundraiser. My family went to church with the Lakes at the time, and it was an awful scandal. I felt so bad for her. She was a lovely woman."

"Mrs. Lake *did* do it?"

Connie nodded. "She did, but it's not that simple. Mr. Lake worked in construction, and he'd had a bad accident earlier in the year—a fall from a ladder that broke a number of bones. He couldn't work anymore, of course. He had to go through several surgeries, and he was on all kinds of painkillers. At that point, it was just the two boys living at home, so Mr. Lake must have been at least sixty when this happened." Connie chuckled. "Isn't that something? He seemed ancient to me then, but *I'm* sixty now."

Hannah grinned. "Isn't it funny how our perception of 'old' changes?"

"It is, indeed. Well, what none of us realized—because the Lakes were very private, self-sufficient people—was that they were in a desperate financial situation. It's not cheap to raise any children, much less eight of them. And now they had all these medical bills and no income. As soon as the school and church realized that Mrs. Lake had taken the money because she was trying to keep the electricity on and feed her boys, lots of people pitched in to help." Connie shook her head. "Mrs. Lake must've had the patience of a saint. First raising six girls, then two boys like Edward and Lincoln."

Hannah raised her eyebrows. "Were the boys hard to manage?"

"They were just mischievous." Connie's eyes twinkled. "They weren't mean-spirited or anything, but they did sow a few wild oats. They turned out okay, though. Whenever I see them in town—in their suits or polo shirts—I want to laugh because they look like the straightest arrows you've ever seen. You'd never know the trouble they used to get into."

"That's a hard thing about living where you grew up," Hannah said. "Everybody knows who you were back in high school."

"I think it's good for us. Keeps us from getting too big for our britches, as my mama always said." Connie dumped several paper plates into a trash bag. "Edward and Lincoln can wear all the fancy suits they want, but to those of us who've lived here a long time, they'll always be the mischievous Lake boys."

After all the preparations for the baby shower, Hannah was delighted when her dad told her they were ordering Chinese food that night. Drew and Allison had volunteered to pick it up on their way over, so all Hannah needed to do was show up. As much as she loved making food, especially for her favorite people, being asked to arrive at a family gathering with nothing but herself felt like a gift.

When Hannah parked in her dad's driveway, she saw over the low backyard fence that the Slip 'N Slide had been set up, and her niece and nephews were running wild. Zeus barked playfully, chasing them along the slide while staying far enough away to avoid the water.

As Hannah let herself in the back gate, she wasn't at all surprised to hear Aunt Fiona's voice ring out, "Clear the way!" a moment before her aunt sprinted through the grass in bare feet and a bright red swimsuit. The kids cheered as Aunt Fiona dove along the slide and came to rest in the shallow pool of water at the end.

"Aunt Hannah!" Ava shrieked as Hannah closed the gate behind her.

A moment later, lukewarm water soaked through Hannah's shorts as her eight-year-old niece squeezed her in a hug.

Axel, age six, called out to Hannah, "It's your turn on the slide!" as he jumped up and down in the shallow pool, splashing water everywhere.

Aunt Fiona laughed and shielded her eyes as she stood.

"Unfortunately, I didn't wear my swimsuit," Hannah said.

"Watch this, Aunt Hannah," called AJ, the oldest at age ten.

Hannah grinned and applauded him as he slid just like Aunt Fiona, popping up at the other end and raising his hands in victory. "Wow, nice job, AJ!"

Aunt Fiona wrapped a towel around herself as she came to greet Hannah. Her silver-streaked hair was wet enough that she'd likely been out there for a while with the kids. "I can't remember the last time I was on a Slip 'N Slide."

"That's hard to believe," Hannah said. "You looked like a professional sliding down at the end."

Aunt Fiona laughed as she rubbed her hair with the towel. "I play softball twice a week on a rec league in DC. The skills translate surprisingly well."

Hannah shook her head, amazed at her aunt's youth and vibrancy. Looking at her now, it was hard to believe that Mom had been this age when she died. Hannah had never thought of her mom as youthful—what child did?—but even so, Mom had been so sick in her final years. That Aunt Fiona was not only here and alive, but also capable of playing on a Slip 'N Slide, should be celebrated.

"What day is your actual birthday?" Hannah asked.

"Friday. I'm still trying to figure out how to spend the day. I have a decent number of high school friends still in town, and of course I want to do something with you and the family."

"What about a party?"

"Oh, I don't need anything like that. Besides, you just finished throwing a party."

Hannah slipped her arm through her aunt's. "I mean it. Friday night, at my place. Invite anybody."

"That's really not necessary, Hannah," Aunt Fiona said.

But her eyes sparkled with delight all the same.

Chapter Six

"Wait, didn't you just throw a party?" Liam asked.

Hannah pressed the phone to her ear as she restocked canned tomatoes in the Hot Spot pantry. "I know. I couldn't help myself, though."

"You do love celebrating others. And I love that about you."

"That is too generous," Hannah said. "Lacy's baby and Aunt Fiona's birthday are events worth celebrating, even if they are so close together. And my aunt's party won't be nearly as involved. My apartment is already party-ready because of the baby shower, and others are going to help with food, so it'll hardly be any work."

"Mm-hmm." Liam's tone said he didn't believe her. "I need to go, but I'll try to call you later, okay?"

"Love you."

"Love you too," Liam said, and the call ended.

Hannah tucked her phone away and quickly wrapped up her work in the Hot Spot storage room. When she entered the dining room a couple minutes later, only a few tables were occupied. Considering it was Tuesday at five o'clock, this wasn't too surprising. She found Elaine at the hostess stand, fussing needlessly with the basket of silverware rolls.

"Do you want to get off your feet for ten or fifteen minutes?" Hannah asked. "Since we're slow?"

Elaine glanced at the sidewalk, seeming hopeful that a herd of customers were about to come in. Everybody who worked at the Hot Spot preferred busy evenings to slow ones. "Are you sure?" Elaine asked.

Hannah smirked and gestured to the sparsely populated dining room. "I think I can handle this."

Elaine laughed. "I'll grab a bite to eat and then I'll be back. Thanks, Hannah."

Hannah leaned against the hostess stand and looked out on the sidewalks of Blackberry Valley. The weather was drizzly, which was good because they needed rain. She knew it was almost ninety degrees outside, but still thought longingly of curling into a chair with a good book and a cup of tea. Or maybe a glass of iced tea.

To her left, a jarring sound yanked Hannah from her thoughts.

At the closest occupied booth, a man who appeared to be in his eighties sat with a clenched fist on the tabletop. His face was flushed, and he glared at the two people who sat across from him, neither of whom Hannah could see from this angle. There was a woman seated beside him that Hannah didn't recognize. She also looked to be in her eighties, though she appeared younger than the man. Or perhaps she was just in better health. The woman lifted a water glass to her mouth and turned away from the angry man beside her, facing out the window.

"You don't understand what you're doing." The man's voice was gravely, more like a growl. "You can't start changing everything all at once or you'll bankrupt the place."

The responding voice was calm and feminine. "Spending a little money on improvements isn't going to bankrupt anyone, Dad."

Hannah couldn't see the speaker's face, only the chestnut-brown of her hair peeking over the top of the high booth.

The man pointed a thick finger at her. "You keep this up, and you will."

"Lawrence, I think you're overreacting." The voice was male and seemed familiar, though Hannah couldn't place it. Nor could she see the man from this vantage point. "Courtney has made a few changes, yes, but—"

"A few changes?" Lawrence pounded his fist on the table, which was definitely the sound Hannah had heard a minute ago. "A *few*?"

The woman beside Lawrence—his wife, Hannah guessed—rested a hand on his arm. Hannah couldn't hear what she said to him, but a moment later, Lawrence said, "How can I be calm when our daughter is spending money like it's nothing?"

Again, the man Hannah couldn't see replied, "That's hardly what Courtney is doing."

"I appreciate you defending me, but I don't need you to fight my battles for me, Lincoln," Courtney said.

Lincoln Lake. *That* was why the voice sounded familiar.

"Dad, I know I'm making different choices than you did when you were running the company, but I believe that investing in our rental properties is money that will come back to us. Many of our buildings have needed updates for years. Making them nicer will—"

"*I* believe that I don't need a lecture from someone who has been in charge of the business for less than a month." Grabbing hold of the cane leaning against the table, Lawrence pushed himself to standing.

Before he could catch her staring, Hannah turned her attention to the hostess stand and pretended to be engrossed in the map of tables.

"Dad." Courtney sounded exasperated. "You're being unreasonable."

"Your father has a doctor's appointment we need to get to," Lawrence's wife said. Hannah heard sounds of her scooting out of the booth as well.

"You don't have to make excuses for him, Mom."

But seconds later, Lawrence came into Hannah's view, barreling toward the front door. His wife trotted along behind him.

"Have a good evening," Hannah said with a practiced smile.

Only the wife acknowledged that Hannah had spoken. She lifted a hand in farewell and then rushed to follow her husband.

Hannah couldn't resist glancing over her shoulder. Courtney had moved to the side of the booth her parents had vacated. She was in her late forties or early fifties, with a round face, a sleek bob of brown hair, and a mouth currently pressed into a grimace. She wore the kind of tailored business suit that Hannah always admired but had no occasion to own.

She slumped back in the booth. "Typical Dad. If he can't control a conversation, he's not going to have it."

Lincoln shifted to the middle of the bench where he sat, and now Hannah could see his graying auburn hair and part of his shoulder, which lifted in a shrug. "Maybe he really did have a doctor's appointment."

Courtney looked at Lincoln over the top of her black glasses. "You know that was a lie. What doctor takes appointments after five in the evening?"

The conversation halted as Raquel arrived carrying a platter of loaded nachos and looking confused.

"My parents had to leave suddenly," Courtney said in a voice that sounded weary. "Is it too late to cancel their entrees?"

"I'll run back there and make sure it happens." Raquel placed the appetizer in the middle of the table. "I hope nothing's wrong."

Courtney chuckled humorlessly. "Only the normal family drama. These look delicious. Thank you."

The front door swung open, and Hannah turned her attention to the family that had just entered, a mom and dad who were each holding a small child. "Hello, welcome to the Hot Spot. Four of you?"

By the time Hannah had seated the young family, another foursome had arrived—this time two couples. Hannah seated them as well and then found Elaine had returned and reclaimed her position at the hostess stand.

Hannah's gaze slid to where the family drama had unfolded and found Lincoln now alone at the booth. On the other side of the window, Courtney paced back and forth on the sidewalk, her phone pressed to her ear.

Lincoln was tapping away at something on his phone, but he looked up as Hannah approached the table. A warm smile slid onto his face.

Hannah returned the smile and paused alongside where he sat. "How's your dinner so far?"

"Great," Lincoln said. He must've seen how Hannah's gaze flicked to Courtney on the sidewalk because he followed the word with a small laugh. "Well, I don't know that *great* is the right word. First, I watched my boss fight with her parents, and now she's on the phone with one of our building managers. But the loaded nachos are excellent as always, and now I have them all to myself."

He made a show of sliding more nachos onto his plate. He was in his fifties, but with his ever-present smile and tanned face, he still had the boyish charm of youth.

"That *is* a positive. Sorry it's been an awkward dinner."

Lincoln shrugged. "This is one of the downsides of working in a family business. There's often squabbling. I've learned that it's best to stay neutral."

Hannah shifted her attention to Courtney, pacing the sidewalk in her pinstriped skirt, blouse, and heels that made Hannah's feet ache to look at them. "I don't recognize your boss."

"Courtney Underhill. She grew up on Lake Blackberry. She's been in Atlanta for the last twenty or so years and recently moved back to take over for her dad. Lawrence doesn't want to admit how bad his health has become, but he's declining quickly."

His words brought to mind the conversation she'd overheard between Elaine and Raquel just a few days before, when Raquel was rejoicing about new management at her apartment complex. Hadn't she said it was the daughter who'd taken over? This must be the family. Based on her limited exposure to them, Hannah could see why Courtney's management style was a welcome change to tenants.

"I'm sorry to hear that," Hannah said. "It's hard to watch someone we care about struggle with their health."

Lincoln gave her a closed-mouth smile and nodded his acceptance of her condolences. She didn't have a hard time imagining that he'd been attractive in his teenage years. Was the potential awkwardness of asking Lincoln her questions a worthwhile risk?

After a moment's debate, Hannah decided yes. "This is an odd question, but did you ever go by Apollo in high school?"

Lincoln blinked at her a few times, understandably confused. "No. Why do you ask?"

"Oh, it's a little silly." Hannah's cheeks heated. "I live upstairs in what used to be the firemen's sleeping quarters, and I found a compass that belonged to someone named Apollo. I was told by Rusty Studebaker that the compass looked like the same ones given to those in the Wayfinders, and he mentioned you were in that group."

"Wow, Hannah." Lincoln leaned onto his elbows. "Rusty Studebaker? Wayfinders? You are taking me back to the good old days."

His reaction helped Hannah not to feel so awkward about her question. "Are you missing your compass?"

Lincoln shook his head. "My wife is incredibly organized, and I know exactly where that compass is—in a box labeled LINCOLN'S CHILDHOOD KEEPSAKES on a shelf in our basement."

"Wow, that's impressive."

"That's my wife in a nutshell—impressive."

How sweet was that? Hannah loved seeing the smile on Lincoln's face as he spoke about Suzanne. Hannah rejoiced whenever she saw spouses who cared deeply about each other.

"Any chance you're still in touch with other Wayfinders?" Hannah asked. "I'd like to return this compass to the owner, whoever he is."

"Only a few of the guys, but I can ask around. It's not my big brother's. His is framed in his office at the city."

"Really?"

Edward had always struck Hannah as being very business-focused and not the type to cherish sentimental items, much less frame and display them.

"Wayfinders was a meaningful experience for both of us. It's hard for me to imagine anybody parting with their compass willingly."

Hannah leaned against the table. "What made the group so special?"

"Kenneth," Lincoln said without hesitation. "He was a remarkable man. He loved people, even rascals who didn't make it easy, like me and Edward. Whenever we'd get in trouble, Kenneth would be there to make sure we took responsibility. Like one time we egged this cranky old woman's house. Kenneth found out and took us back to her place. After we cleaned up the mess, he made us rake her lawn and weed her garden."

Hannah marveled that Kenneth had held the boys accountable and that Lincoln loved him for it. "That's amazing."

Lincoln nodded. "Now that I have my own teenagers, I wonder how he found time to invest in us on top of parenting his own kids, plus being a husband and fireman. We went on hikes once a month and learned how to do things like build a fire and set up a tent. He took us backpacking a couple times. Some of my best memories are from my Wayfinder days. I'll ask around and see if any of the guys are missing their compasses."

In her peripheral vision, Hannah spotted Courtney approaching the table and turned to greet her with a smile. "Hello. I'm Hannah, the owner of the Hot Spot."

"Hi, Hannah." Courtney held out a hand. "Courtney Underhill. Nice to meet you."

Hannah was unsurprised by Courtney's firm handshake. "Lincoln was just telling me that you've recently moved back to Blackberry Valley."

"That's right," Courtney said. "And I love your restaurant."

Hannah beamed at the unexpected compliment. "Thank you. That's so kind." She stepped to the side as Raquel approached with a tray bearing two entrees.

"Sorry it took longer than usual." Raquel glanced at Hannah, as if she thought that might be why Hannah was at the table.

"No need to apologize," Courtney said as she slid into the booth. "Gave me a chance to have it out with my father and then straighten out one of our property managers."

"You've had a very productive wait time," Hannah said. "And I'm fairly sure that Raquel is one of your tenants, Courtney."

"Oh, really?" Courtney's dark brown eyes lit with interest. "Where do you live, Raquel?"

"At the corner of Juliette and Third Street."

"I adore that building." Courtney rested a hand over her heart. "It's one of my favorites. We just had that parking lot repaved."

Raquel grinned. "It's wonderful. Thank you so much for doing that."

"It was selfish. I felt like I was off-roading in my Jeep when I drove through it the first time." Courtney gestured to a bright yellow Jeep Wrangler parallel-parked out the window. "I apologize for how overdue it was. There are more changes to come, I assure you. Now that I'm in charge."

Raquel couldn't have smiled any bigger if she'd tried, but Hannah was pretty sure she caught sight of a frown on Lincoln's face right before he took a large bite.

Chapter Seven

Wednesday morning dawned warm and humid enough that the mere idea of drinking hot coffee made Hannah sweat. After pulling a baseball cap over her sleep-rumpled hair and setting out the unbaked cinnamon rolls she'd placed in the refrigerator overnight, she trekked to Jump Start for an iced coffee, which she brought back to her apartment.

While the oven heated, she allowed herself a few minutes to sit and sip in refreshing silence, then she made herself get to work preparing her place for Aunt Fiona's party on Friday night. The furniture in her apartment was already set for a party. After the baby shower, she'd left the couch pushed into the corner to make space for extra chairs. The end tables were already free of clutter and held only stacks of extra coasters. The farm-themed baby decorations needed to come down, though.

Hannah wanted to run to the party supply store to find something fun to celebrate Aunt Fiona, but a glance at her phone told her there wasn't time, even if she didn't have cinnamon rolls in the oven. She was due at her dad's house at ten o'clock for brunch. But there was time to take down the baby shower decorations and clear the pile of mail in her kitchen while the rolls baked.

As she sorted a mixture of personal and restaurant mail, Hannah uncovered a Blackberry Valley High School yearbook from

1986. She stared at it for a moment before remembering that this copy was Suzanne Lake's, which Lacy had brought to the baby shower and left behind for her to peruse. The cinnamon rolls still had five more minutes in the oven, and they needed cooling time before she drizzled the icing over them, so Hannah set aside the mail and opened the yearbook.

The fluffy bangs and oversized glasses made Hannah grin. Her own yearbook probably looked dated too—she'd graduated nearly twenty years ago—but surely not as dated as *this*.

When the timer for the rolls startled her a few minutes later, she remembered she wasn't supposed to be giggling about perms and flipped-up collars, but looking for Sunflower and Apollo.

As the rolls cooled on the counter, Hannah spotted a few names she recognized in the freshman class, including Rusty Studebaker and Lincoln Lake. She kept running her finger down the list of names, searching for any possible links to Apollo or Sunflower, then paused on the name Fiona Western. Her gaze skimmed over the black-and-white squares until it landed on a young image of her aunt.

Because she knew it was Aunt Fiona, she could see glimmers of the woman she knew—the shape of the eyes, the slant of her cheekbones, the blondness of her hair—but the demeanor was all wrong. Instead of the sparkling, warm eyes and the wide, easy smile, teenage Fiona appeared demure, maybe even timid. Young Fiona stared into the camera with a serious expression, her mouth only slightly upturned at the corners. How unlikely it seemed that this shy-looking girl would grow up to live all over the country, to laugh easily, and to play on Slip 'N Slides well into her fifties.

Hannah glanced at the clock and found that it was 9:55. "Whoops!"

She hastily added icing to the cinnamon rolls, then scooped the yearbook into her purse, grabbed the pan with a couple of oven mitts, and rushed out to her car.

"I was beginning to wonder if you forgot about us," Dad greeted her from the doorway. But he was grinning, as was Aunt Fiona, who stood behind him.

Hannah's hands were occupied with the pan of cinnamon rolls, plus she had the 1986 yearbook trapped between her elbow and her side, so she pushed her car door shut with her foot. "Sorry, I got distracted. It was actually Aunt Fiona's fault."

"No surprise there," Aunt Fiona said with a laugh. "That's usually the case. What'd I do this time?"

"I was looking through this." Hannah angled her body so Aunt Fiona could see the yearbook.

Aunt Fiona cocked her head and then released a loud laugh. She pulled the yearbook from beneath Hannah's elbow. "This was in 1986? Oh no. I think that was the year I got my perm."

"You're definitely rocking some classic eighties hair in your yearbook photo," Hannah called over her shoulder as she carried the pan into the kitchen.

Uncle Gordon stood at the stove, frying sausage patties. He grinned at her. "How's my Hannah Banana today? Ooh, cinnamon rolls."

"That's right." Hannah eased them onto the counter. "Fresh from the oven."

"There's nothing better than that."

Aunt Fiona walked into the kitchen, giggling as she pointed at the yearbook. "Look at this. I'm so awkward."

"You're not," Hannah protested. "You're just young."

"I was so solemn back then. I hadn't come out of my shell yet, as the saying goes."

Uncle Gordon gaped at Aunt Fiona. "Wait, did you used to be *shy*?"

"Absurdly shy." Aunt Fiona smiled indulgently at the image of her younger self. "I wish I could hug this girl and tell her she doesn't have to take everything so seriously. Bless her heart."

Uncle Gordon turned off the burner and shuttled sausages onto a plate lined with a paper towel. "What I wouldn't give to have the wisdom I have now, but the body and energy I had at eighteen."

"Isn't that the truth?" Dad agreed.

Hannah's heart felt light and happy as they filled their plates with cinnamon rolls, sausage, and fruit salad, then sat around the same table where she'd eaten most meals as a girl. Aunt Fiona continued to flip through the yearbook pages and call out names, and the three older people discussed Blackberry Valley families of years gone by. Hannah didn't have much to contribute to the conversation, but that was okay with her. She felt delighted to be in the same room as these people she loved, soaking up their stories.

She regretted that she hadn't done more of this when her mom was alive. She hadn't been wise enough at the time to know that the opportunity to hear these kinds of stories wouldn't last forever.

"I'm so glad you brought this," Aunt Fiona said an hour later. Their plates had long been empty, but they lingered at the table. Aunt Fiona hugged the yearbook to her chest. "Mine are buried in boxes that I haven't unpacked for the last few moves. I should get them out again."

Hannah loved that something so simple had made her aunt this happy. She stood and began gathering plates. Dad and Uncle Gordon chatted as they put the leftover food away. "I'm happy to have provided entertainment for you this morning."

"You certainly did." Aunt Fiona's expression changed as though a thought had just occurred to her. "Why on earth do you have a 1986 yearbook lying around?"

"Oh, that's a funny story actually." Hannah rested the stacked plates on the table. "I'm surprised I haven't told you yet. While I was cleaning my apartment, I noticed a loose brick in the wall. I pulled it out, and I found a compass and a note from 1986 back there. The note looked like something a teenager had written, but neither Lacy nor I recognized the names, so she borrowed a yearbook in hopes that we'd find them."

"Well, that's odd." Aunt Fiona stood and gathered the remaining silverware and napkins from the table. "What were their names? Maybe I know them."

"We think they were actually nicknames, but do you know anyone who went by Sunflower or Apollo in high school?"

Aunt Fiona froze. Her green eyes locked on Hannah, wide and unblinking.

Hannah's heart rate spiked. "You do, don't you?"

"I'd like to see what you found behind the brick." Her aunt's voice was low and a touch raspy. "I'd like to see it right now."

Blackberry Valley High School
October 3, 1985

Fiona Western stared with horror at her history teacher as he used some of her least favorite phrases to describe how they'd spend class time today: They'd be given a partner—yuck—to work on a collaborative project—no thank you—which would be presented to the class. That was the worst part of it all.

Tears pricked her eyes. She liked to work alone, and giving presentations was the stuff of her nightmares. She'd have to stand in front of the blackboard with all those eyes on her. She'd have to speak at an audible volume. Teachers were always admonishing her for being too quiet when she talked.

At least the teacher was picking partners for them. Fiona wouldn't have to endure the agony of finding a partner in a class where she had no close friends. Which just meant a class where she didn't have Jennifer, because Jennifer was her only close friend.

The teacher started reading off pairs of names along with the Revolutionary War era event they were assigned. "Fiona Western" was spoken alongside "Theo Drakos" and "Boston Tea Party."

Fiona gulped. Theo was the new boy. He seemed nice enough, as far as boys went. He smiled a lot and answered teachers' questions intelligently but without appearing to love the sound of his own voice. While Fiona knew she could've been assigned a worse partner, her stomach twisted with dread as Theo approached her desk.

"You're Fiona, right?"

"Yes." The word had barely made a sound. She cleared her throat and tried again. "Yes."

"Cool." Theo dropped into the chair beside her. "I'm Theo."

Fiona nodded. She met Theo's eyes for one brave moment—long enough to know they were dark, but not long enough to discern the actual color—and then looked away.

"So." Theo opened his textbook. "Do you have ideas of how we should do this?"

Fiona kept her eyes on her own book. She did, but she shrugged.

He laughed. "I'm not sure I believe that."

Theo's response—warm but direct—was such a surprise that Fiona forgot to keep her eyes down.

He grinned, and his cheeks went a bit pink. "I've noticed you don't say much, but when you do, it's good stuff. If you knew the answer to that question yesterday in biology, I'm sure you have ideas of the best way to do this assignment."

Fiona's mind couldn't get beyond those first three words of his—*I've noticed you.* He'd noticed her? Fiona worked very hard not to be noticed. The only reason she'd answered that question was because their science teacher was the sort who called on kids instead of asking for raised hands.

"Well." Fiona wiped her sweaty hands on her jeans. "I guess I think we should start by reading the section independently?"

Why had she said it that way? *I guess I think.* What did that even mean? And why had the sentence curled into a question at the end? That wasn't how she meant it.

But Theo didn't seem to notice. "We can each take notes on key points and then compare lists when we're done. Sound good?"

Fiona murmured, "Yes," and they both silently read what the textbook had to say about the Boston Tea Party. Doing this took longer than it should have because she kept thinking about Theo's words: *I've noticed you.*

Even so, she was done before Theo.

When he finished a few minutes later, he gave her a rueful smile. "Sorry. I'm a slow reader."

She felt herself smiling back at him without realizing she was going to do it, same as she would if she was with Jennifer or her sister, Frieda. "That's okay. I think you took more notes than I did, though."

She'd spoken two sentences at an audible volume. This was going well.

Theo slid his notebook close to hers so they could compare and compile. His handwriting was tight and neat on the page.

"About the presentation tomorrow," Theo said. The words sent a rush of hot anxiety through Fiona. "What if we start with you sharing our topic, and then these two points?"

With his pen, Theo touched the two that would require the least amount of speaking.

Even so, Fiona's mouth was dry. She nodded and attempted a smile.

Theo looked back to their notebooks. "We could do it differently if you want."

She shook her head. She was having a hard time looking at him.

"If I thought we could get away with you not presenting, I'd be cool with that." His voice was low and kind. "But your grade would take a hit."

He was being so nice to her. Usually in group projects, Fiona's shyness meant one of two things happened—she got stuck with all the work, or she was given the worst jobs because everybody else spoke up quickly and took the best for themselves.

"I have a hard time..." Her gaze traveled to the front of the room, where she'd have to stand tomorrow.

"I figured. You remind me of my mom." Theo tipped his chair back on two legs while twirling a pencil. "She's really nervous in groups or with people she doesn't know, but when she's comfortable with someone, she's the best."

Fiona felt her sharp intake of air. Theo was not saying that she, Fiona, was the best. He was just comparing his mom's nervous nature to her own. This was nothing to get excited about.

"Maybe try looking at the back of the room instead of at people?" Theo suggested, bringing his chair to rest on all four legs. "My mom says that helps her. Or I could stand over to the side while you present, and then you can look at me while you're talking. You can pretend I'm that friend of yours. The one with the big bangs."

"Jennifer?"

Theo fluffed the front of his curly, dark hair and made an attempt to position it on his forehead like Jennifer's bangs. "How's that?"

Fiona heard herself giggling and was so surprised that she did it again. "That's pretty good."

Theo grinned at her and then attempted to smooth his dark hair back into place. The curls didn't lay quite the same as they had before he'd brushed them out.

While his attention was elsewhere, Fiona took a moment to study Theo's long, dark lashes and his olive skin tone. Even though his heavy brows and long nose kept him from being traditionally handsome, when he smiled at her, she thought Apollo himself couldn't hold a candle to Theo Drakos.

Chapter Eight

Aunt Fiona was silent the entire drive to Hannah's apartment. It was so unusual that Hannah felt asking any questions would be disrespectful, so she left Aunt Fiona to her own thoughts.

Once they'd entered Hannah's apartment, she retrieved the compass and note from her bedroom dresser, then handed them to Aunt Fiona. "Here."

Aunt Fiona sank onto the couch. She unfolded the note and stared. Seconds ticked by, then a minute.

Finally, she took in a deep, shaky breath. "I apologize for my reticence, Hannah." She placed the note on the coffee table as though it were made of delicate glass. "The note was written by me. *I'm* Sunflower."

With her aunt's intense reaction, Hannah had suspected this. She laced her fingers together on her lap. "Who was Apollo?"

"A friend of mine in high school. His name was Theo." Aunt Fiona studied the compass. "This belonged to him too. He was part of a group called Wayfinders. Have you heard of them?"

Hannah nodded. "As I understand it, there was a fireman who mentored teenage boys and did various outdoor activities with them. Similar to the Boy Scouts."

"That's right. Theo absolutely loved it. To think he didn't take his compass with him..." Aunt Fiona's eyes were full of unshed tears. "Can you show me where you found this?"

Hannah went over to the wall and demonstrated how the loose brick came out.

"Hmm." Aunt Fiona stared at the compass. She ran her thumb over the casing again and again, as if doing so would cause the hand to point to answers.

Hannah joined her aunt on the couch. "Do you have ideas about why Theo would've left the compass and your note here at the fire station?"

"I can venture a guess, but I don't know for sure."

Hannah laid a hand over her aunt's. "You don't have to tell me anything if you don't want to. I'm curious, but I won't pry."

Aunt Fiona looked at the compass a moment longer before placing it on top of the note. "Theo lived with his mom on the outskirts of town. These days it's Lake Blackberry, with a beautiful park and all those big, fancy houses and docks. But back in the eighties it wasn't anything like that. The house he lived in was an old two-bedroom house they rented. I was only there a couple times."

"Is it there now?"

Aunt Fiona's lips thinned. "No. The summer between our sophomore and junior years—a few weeks after I wrote that letter to him—their house burned down."

"Oh." Hannah hadn't expected a *happy* story based on Aunt Fiona's body language, but she hadn't imagined something as dramatic as a house fire. "Was everyone all right?"

"Yes, thankfully." Aunt Fiona sent Hannah a reassuring smile. "Neither Theo nor his mom were home at the time. It happened on the Fourth of July, so they were in town for the celebration."

"What a relief. How did the house catch fire?"

"I'm not sure, actually. Some thought it was an errant firework. It's not uncommon for people to shoot off fireworks outside the city limits." She gave a wry smile. "Or even *in* city limits, back in my day. But most people thought Ivy, Theo's mom, was responsible."

Hannah noted the set of Aunt Fiona's jaw and thought of how vehemently she'd spoken of Theo's mom in her note to him—*I will defend her to anyone who I hear saying those horrible things.* Obviously, that wasn't about the fire because the note was written before the Fourth of July, but Aunt Fiona had thought highly of Ivy, and that was enough for Hannah to do so as well.

"But you didn't think so?" Hannah asked.

Aunt Fiona tipped her head from side to side, as if weighing the options. "I'm really not sure. Ivy was a different sort of person. She was eccentric, but I liked her a lot. She could get lost in her own head at times. Theo used to tell me stories of coming home from school and finding water boiling on the stove, even though his mom had already left for work. Whenever she left the house, he walked around and made sure that she hadn't left water running or her curling iron on or anything like that."

"That sounds really stressful."

"I'm sure it was, though he never talked about her as if she were a burden." Aunt Fiona nodded to the note folded on the table. "If my memory can be trusted, when I wrote that note to Theo, there were rumors going around town that his mom had sold bundles of poison ivy at the farmer's market. It was nothing more than small-town gossip. Not only was Ivy a single mother, but she was also shy and a bit odd." The corners of Aunt Fiona's mouth twitched downward. "She was probably very lonely."

"Why did you and Theo use nicknames?" Hannah asked.

"Just for fun," Aunt Fiona said with a fond smile. "I had a shirt with a sunflower on it that I wore a lot, plus my hair was blond, so Theo started calling me Sunflower. I decided he needed a nickname too."

Hannah didn't think she was imagining the rising color in her aunt's cheeks. "And Apollo is what you chose?"

"Theo was Greek. And very tall." Aunt Fiona shrugged, but her cheeks were definitely pink. "Apollo seemed to fit him. Like I said, it was a silly inside joke with a friend. We mostly used them when we wrote notes to each other during class."

"Of course," Hannah said, deciding not to press the issue.

Aunt Fiona reached for the compass again and held it reverently in her palm. "Theo's father died when he was really young. I think that's why Wayfinders meant so much to him. He didn't have a dad to teach him how to build a campfire or fish or anything like that. Kenneth Cutuli filled that gap for him."

"Kenneth sounds like an amazing man."

"I didn't know him well, but I think he was." Aunt Fiona's inhale was shaky. "Aside from my parents and Frieda, I'm not sure anybody has had as big an impact on me as Theo did. I was debilitatingly shy as a child, and Theo was the one who reached me. Who showed me how to stop hiding. How to let people see me." Her eyes shone with tears. "Theo means 'gift from God,' and he really was that to me. I wouldn't be who I am without him."

Hannah waited for Aunt Fiona to continue, but minutes ticked by in silence. Finally, Hannah asked in a gentle voice, "So what happened?"

Blackberry Valley
July 8, 1986

"I mean, I don't know for sure that he likes me, but it does seem like he's going out of his way to talk to me." Frieda adjusted her hands on the steering wheel of her Ford Tempo. "Maybe I'm reading too much into this. Maybe it means nothing."

Fiona gazed at her beautiful, outgoing sister. "I don't think so. It's pretty obvious that Gabriel Prentiss is interested in you."

"Really?" Frieda glanced at her, then returned her attention to the road. "You're not just saying that?"

Fiona rolled her eyes. Her sister had moved back to Blackberry Valley a month ago to take a teaching job at the elementary school this fall. In the last month, Fiona had witnessed no less than six times that Gabriel Prentiss had come up with excuses to stop by and talk to Frieda.

"Not at all," Fiona said. "I'm positive Gabriel didn't 'happen' to drive by the house this morning. I think he remembered that you said we'd be getting back from the family reunion last night, and he probably drove by the house a hundred times hoping to catch you coming out to your car."

"Don't be ridiculous," Frieda said, her face a pretty shade of pink.

Fiona grinned. Their entire childhood, Frieda had longed to be a wife and mother, but hadn't dated much. Fiona would love to see Frieda happily dating somebody, especially if it was somebody like Gabriel who would likely keep her in Blackberry Valley.

"Now, tell me about this Theo of yours," Frieda said, taking her eyes off the gravel road to smile at her sister.

"He's not *my* Theo." Fiona felt her cheeks turn hot. She looked down at the bag of saltwater taffy that she'd brought back from the beach for him. "We're just good friends."

"Oh, really?" Frieda's tone made it clear she didn't believe this at all.

"Yes," Fiona said. "Really."

"Mom says he's brought you out of your shell."

"I don't like the two of you talking about me behind my back." Fiona looked out the window as the Kentucky countryside flew by. Theo lived so far out of town that she couldn't just ride her bike to his house, which was why she'd asked Frieda to drive her out here.

"If you would actually tell me stuff, I wouldn't have to get my information from Mom. You like him, right?"

Fiona's insides squirmed. "We're very good friends. And this is your turn."

Frieda groaned loudly and lifted her foot off the accelerator. "Don't give me that 'good friends' line. I'm your sister. I see how you light up whenever his name is mentioned."

Fiona bit her lip. Of course she liked Theo. How could she not? But Theo was friends with lots of girls at school, and Fiona never noticed him treating her any differently than he did them. Fiona reminded him of his mom, he had said early on in their friendship, and what boy wanted to date a girl who reminded him of his mom?

Fiona's tummy swooped as Frieda crested the hill with gusto and Lake Blackberry came into view. "I wouldn't say no if he asked me on a date or something, but the thing is..." Fiona's gaze drifted down the hill, toward Theo's house.

Or where Theo's house *should* be.

"The thing is?" Frieda prompted her.

But Fiona couldn't speak. Lake Blackberry was where it always was, with the sun glinting off its still waters, but there was no small, yellow house in front of it. There were only charred remains of what had once been Theo's home.

Chapter Nine

Blackberry Valley
July 8, 1986

Fiona suspected she was annoying her mother, staring at her while she spoke on the phone with Mrs. Cutuli, but she couldn't help it. Mom held the kitchen phone to her ear, stretching the cord this way and that as she prepared a spaghetti dinner. Mom kept saying things like, "Oh, dear," and "Really?" which made Fiona want to scream with frustration. She'd begged her mom to be able to listen to the call from the extension in her parents' bedroom, but Mom said that would be rude to Mrs. Cutuli, and that Fiona would just have to wait.

But they'd been on the phone for nearly half an hour, and Fiona was in agony.

"I'm so sorry to hear that," Mom said. "What a tragedy."

For a moment, Fiona couldn't breathe. "Is he dead?" she asked in a raspy voice.

Mom shook her head, and Fiona's lungs released the breath she'd been holding.

The phone call lasted another excruciating five minutes before Mom finally said, "I really appreciate this, Joan. Fiona has been beside herself since she saw the house this morning. Thank you so much. Good night."

"What'd she say?" Fiona asked.

Mom held out the handset. "Hang this up for me, will you?"

Fiona did as Mom asked and then returned to the stove. "What happened?"

Mom fixed her with a look of such sadness that Fiona's throat cinched tight. This wouldn't be good news. She'd known that, of course, because a burned-down house could never be good news, but even so.

Mom turned the burner to low. "Let's sit."

Fiona swallowed hard and took a seat at the round kitchen table where they'd eaten meals all her life. Mom took the seat beside her and reached for Fiona's hands. Even without knowing what Mom was going to say, she could feel the tears welling.

"Theo and his mother are both alive and well. But on the Fourth of July, while everyone was at the city park, a fire started at the Drakoses' house. The place was burned and gone before firefighters could even get there."

Fiona nodded rapidly. "But Theo and Ivy are okay?"

"Yes." Her mom's smile looked forced. "Everything in the house is lost, but Theo and Ivy weren't there. They're safe."

"How did the fire start?"

"That's still being investigated. Mrs. Cutuli said she couldn't talk about it, but that there were several potential causes."

"Did Mrs. Cutuli know if the Drakoses are staying at a hotel?" Fiona asked. Money was tight for them, and that would be a hard expense to bear. "Or are they staying with someone?"

"They stayed with the Cutulis for a few days." Mom swallowed, and her gaze fell to her lap. "But now they're living with Ivy's brother."

"Ivy's brother," Fiona echoed. That made no sense. "But they don't have any family in town."

"That's right, honey." Mom looked her in the eye, regret etched into her face. "I'm so sorry, Fiona, but Theo and his mom have moved to Lexington."

Hannah and Lacy stood in the aisle of the party supply store, Lacy leaning heavily on the cart for support. "Your aunt had no idea that the fire had happened?"

Hannah's eyes were on the brightly colored streamers, but her thoughts were on the conversation yesterday with her aunt. "Aunt Fiona and my grandparents were out of town over the Fourth of July, and you have to remember this was 1986. She wouldn't have had friends texting or calling her to tell her what happened. She wouldn't have seen it on social media. Apparently, Aunt Fiona asked my mom to give her a ride out to Theo's house the first morning they were home, and the house was a pile of ashes."

"Poor Fiona. And she never saw him again?"

"Never." Hannah selected yellow, orange, and red streamers to weave together. The colors were bright and warm, just like her aunt. Though when Hannah had taken her back to Dad's house, Aunt Fiona hadn't been her typical sunny self. Understandably.

"Has she tried to find him?" Lacy asked, trailing behind Hannah as she moved down to the balloons. "She should look on the internet."

Hannah smiled over her shoulder at her best friend. "That's what I said, and Aunt Fiona said she has. She said it looks like Theo lives in Louisville, but he doesn't have any social media accounts that she can find. So, that's it."

"But there was an address?"

Hannah hadn't asked. "I don't think my aunt is keen on the idea of just showing up at Theo's door. She didn't go into details and I didn't press, but it sounds as though she tried hard to get ahold of him for a while and that didn't go well."

Lacy frowned. "What do you mean, it 'didn't go well'? Did she or did she not get ahold of him?"

Hannah tossed a package of yellow balloons into the shopping cart. "That's what she said. 'I did everything I could to get ahold of him, and that didn't go well.'"

Lacy's frown persisted. "Does that mean she never spoke to him? Or that she *did* speak to him and he was a churl about it?"

Hannah was reaching for another balloon package but paused to gape at Lacy. "What on earth is a *churl*?"

"A rude or boorish person. Neil has a word-a-day calendar, and he reads them each day to the baby." Lacy patted her stomach. "I guess I'm picking up on a few as well."

"Of course he's already doing vocab words with the baby. That's maybe the most Neil thing I've ever heard." Hannah surveyed the contents of the cart. "Are plates the last thing on the list?"

"Plates and napkins."

"Thank you. One aisle over, I think."

"Did Fiona ever find out what caused the fire?" Lacy asked as she pushed the cart beside Hannah. "Or did she say why Theo's compass and note would've been hidden in the firehouse?"

"She said Theo was at the firehouse often to see Kenneth, the man who led Wayfinders. Why Theo would've hidden them or when he hid them are both still mysteries, but Aunt Fiona thinks Theo would have had opportunities to do so."

"Must've been sometime between June 7 and July 7, it sounds like," Lacy said. "After your aunt wrote the note, but before Theo left town."

"Yeah, I guess so. As for what caused the fire, Aunt Fiona said most people assumed Ivy was responsible. She was eccentric and could be absent-minded. Theo used to tell Fiona stories about finding curling irons or oven burners left on. But Aunt Fiona thinks even if it was Ivy who burned the house down, it was purely accidental."

"Of course it was. Why would anyone intentionally burn their house down?" Lacy nodded at a colorful display of plates. "There you go."

Hannah wrinkled her nose. "Those are too flimsy. I like the thicker ones that have divided sections, like what I used at your baby shower."

Lacy blinked at her. "Leave it to you to be picky about disposable plates."

"Nobody likes eating on too-small, thin plates, even if they do match the party decor." Hannah pressed on down the aisle. "Back to the fire. Aunt Fiona said there were a few witnesses who said they saw fireworks being shot off that evening near Lake Blackberry, and that might've been the cause. I guess in the eighties Lake Blackberry was really rural, so even if someone was shooting off fireworks, it wasn't like there were a ton of people around to see who or where or anything."

"That's hard to imagine now. All those big houses out there? I've heard the homeowners association is so strict, you have to submit for approval when you want to paint your house, and then the committee decides if the colors are suitable."

"The Lake Blackberry of today is as different as possible from the Lake Blackberry of Aunt Fiona's day. She said Theo and his mom lived in a small, poorly maintained rental house on an acre lot. Lake Blackberry didn't become a desirable place to live until the late eighties when they developed the park along the lake and the country club went in."

"I think the last time I was there was when Margo Carpenter had us all out for a sleepover in seventh grade. Remember that?"

"I remember her bedroom had a balcony, and I'd never been more jealous in my life," Hannah said with a laugh. "That seemed like the height of elegance when we were thirteen. Ooh, *these* plates. This is what I want."

Hannah reached into the bin for several packages of plates that were thick and wouldn't sag or dissolve beneath food. After grabbing a package of yellow napkins, she declared, "Okay, that's it. We can check out now."

The line was unusually long, and Lacy again leaned heavily on the shopping cart.

Hannah cast a nervous glance at her friend. "Do you want to go wait in the car?"

"No, this is good. It's just nice to take the weight off my back for a little bit." Lacy shifted her weight from foot to foot. "I wonder if the fire department has records on old fires. If so, maybe the determined cause is listed in there."

That was a good idea. "I bet you're right."

"Like always." Lacy winked at her. "If only there was someone at the fire department you could ask for help."

"We're in the process of digitizing our records," Liam said when Hannah asked him that afternoon. "But I'm not sure how far back they go. If it's not in the digital records, we'll have paper copies in the storage room. I can have Colt take a look for you."

Hannah plopped into a booth in the empty restaurant. She had a video call with Rusty in five minutes, and the lighting out here was much nicer than in her office. "That'd be nice, thank you. Not a big rush, of course."

"I need to call into the station later today anyway. I'll mention it to him then. How are you? Did you ever talk to the caterer in Glasgow?"

Hannah groaned. With Lacy's baby shower and her aunt's arrival, she'd forgotten to follow up on the potential caterer for the wedding. Supposedly the food was great, but thus far she had been playing phone tag with the owner for two weeks, which didn't seem very promising.

"Not yet."

"Do you want me to call her? I know we agreed that you would be in charge of this, but you have a lot going on right now."

"It's okay." Hannah smoothed hair that didn't need smoothing. "I'll try calling again. Or maybe I'll just cater—"

He cut her off. "No. You are *not* catering our wedding. You are the bride, Hannah Prentiss."

"I'm aware I'm the bride." Hannah checked her watch and opened her laptop. "Doesn't being the bride mean I should get what I want?"

Liam's chuckle made her feel pleasantly warm. "Yes, but you do not want to cater our wedding. Not really. The reality is that you're tired of trying to connect with the place in Glasgow."

"Yes, you're right," Hannah said on an exhale. "I'll try again after I get off my call with Rusty."

"How do you like having a bookkeeper?"

"It's been less than two weeks, so I don't know for sure, but I think I love it." She opened her laptop and typed in her password. "But I haven't had to pay him yet, so check back with me at the end of the month."

"Fair enough. I'll call you again tonight."

"Sounds great. Unless you're too busy packing your bags to come home. Then you don't have to call."

Liam's sigh sounded wistful. "Hopefully soon."

"Hopefully."

After exchanging "I love you" and "goodbye," Hannah hung up feeling a bit melancholy. She bowed her head and said a prayer for the safety of Liam and Archer, as well as a request for favorable conditions for containing the wildfire. She'd just finished when her notification popped up that it was time for her call.

When she logged on, Rusty was already there. He grinned widely at her. "Hello, Hannah." He made a show of observing her surroundings. "Looks like business is slow today."

Hannah laughed and moved out of the frame slightly so Rusty could get an even better view of all the empty tables. "Yeah, I'm not sure I can afford to hire a bookkeeper."

"Maybe I can help you turn things around." Rusty winked at her. "Oh, look, you have a customer. I'm already being helpful."

Hannah turned, ready to wave at whichever of her employees had arrived but instead found her aunt Fiona had come through the door.

"I thought I'd pop in to—" Aunt Fiona saw Hannah was in a meeting and covered her mouth. "I'm so sorry. I'll go wait over here." Her face brightened. "Rusty?"

"No way. Fiona Western?"

Aunt Fiona came closer to the computer and bent so that her face was in the frame, her head hovering around Hannah's shoulder. "How are you?"

"Doing great. Just enjoying a meeting with your wonderful niece. How are you?"

Aunt Fiona's hands rested on Hannah's shoulders. "I'm in town to spend time with my wonderful niece, so no complaints from me. How do you two know each other?"

"I've recently hired Rusty to do the books for the Hot Spot."

"That's excellent." Aunt Fiona pointed at the computer screen. "Rusty and I were always in the same math class, despite him being a grade behind me. I still remember that nightmare unit about exponents. I thought it was going to kill me. If it wasn't for Rusty Studebaker, I might still be in tenth grade."

Rusty's face was pinker than usual. "That's an exaggeration. You just needed a little extra coaching."

Aunt Fiona rolled her eyes at him. "*That* is an exaggeration. Or an understatement, rather. We should get together while I'm in town. I haven't had a chance to meet your wife yet. Maybe Hannah can help us out and share our contact info."

"Sure," Hannah said, unlocking her phone.

"Great. I'll let the two of you have your meeting. Hannah, I'll wait in your office for you."

Hannah tapped her phone screen a few times. "Sounds good. I've shared your phone numbers."

"Got it," Rusty confirmed, his eyes on his phone. He smiled into the camera. "I'll check Pamela's schedule and let you know what works best for having you over. Good to see you, Fiona."

"You too." Aunt Fiona waved one more time and then disappeared in the direction of Hannah's office.

"That was a treat," Rusty said. "I knew the two of you were related, of course, but I didn't realize she was in town. I can't remember the last time I saw your aunt outside of social media. She's always doing something interesting, isn't she?"

Hannah beamed. "That's my aunt. It's been wonderful having her in town." A brilliant idea struck her. "Actually, I'm throwing a birthday party for her tomorrow night. If you're free, you and Pamela should come."

"Oh, I don't want to impose."

"You wouldn't be imposing at all. It'll be upstairs in my apartment from six until the Hot Spot closes. People are free to come and go as they want." Hannah leaned forward on her elbows. "I know Aunt Fiona has invited a few friends from high school, but if you know of anybody else in the area who would like to see her and celebrate her birthday, please feel free to invite them. I'd love it if we basically had a Blackberry Valley High School reunion happening here tomorrow night."

Chapter Ten

Blackberry Valley
August 1, 1986

"Fiona, you're overthinking this."

Fiona looked up from the telephone resting on her lap. The telephone she'd been staring at for at least five minutes. Clutched in her hand was a square of paper with a phone number on it. By now the paper had gone limp because Fiona had held it for so long with her sweaty palms.

"I'm really nervous," she confessed.

Frieda sank onto the arm of the chair. "Theo is your friend, isn't he?"

Fiona hesitated, and hated that she did so. Was she still "friends" with someone if something huge and traumatic happened, but they never told her about it? If they moved without saying goodbye? If they left no way to contact them and didn't try to call her?

Fiona made herself nod. "He's my best friend."

At least that *had* been true.

"Then what do you have to be afraid of?"

Fiona looked up at her big sister. That was easy for Frieda to say, since everybody loved her. Frieda smiled and laughed easily. She didn't act nervous and weird around new people. She never would've been in this situation, because if Theo had been friends with Frieda, he would've made sure she knew how to get ahold of him. Nobody would want to lose someone like Frieda.

"I *will* call him." Fiona tried to keep the bite of annoyance out of her voice and knew from Frieda's recoil that she'd failed. "I'm just thinking through what I'm going to say is all. Words aren't easy for all of us, you know."

Frieda pursed her lips and stood from the arm of the couch. "Okay, fine. I'll be in our bathroom if you need me."

Probably getting ready for another date with Gabriel. Fiona had lost track of how many dates they had gone on in the last few weeks.

Fiona ran her thumb once more over the phone number she'd gotten from Kenneth Cutuli. She'd been mortified to ask an adult if he knew how to contact Theo, but she had run out of options. She'd already asked everyone she could think of, including the boys in Wayfinders and on Theo's baseball team. Nobody knew how to get in touch with him, which Fiona found oddly comforting. It wasn't *just* her who had been shut out, anyway.

Each of the Wayfinder boys told her the same thing: *He stayed at Kenneth's. If anyone knows how to reach Theo, it's him.*

And so Fiona had gathered her courage, knocked on the door of the fire station, and asked Kenneth if he had contact information for Theo. She could barely look him in the eye, but he'd smiled kindly and given her a phone number. "That's the number for his uncle's house in Lexington. I'm not sure they're still there, but that's what I have."

Now the only obstacle in Fiona's way was herself. She inhaled deeply and lifted the receiver to her ear. As she exhaled, she punched in the numbers.

She could do this. This was Theo. Apollo. Her best friend. The one who had known how to talk to her even when she was debilitatingly shy. Theo would be happy to hear from her. He would have some kind of explanation for why he hadn't called her. And then Fiona would say that she understood and—

"Hello?" The voice that answered was female, but it didn't sound like Ivy. His aunt, maybe?

"Hi. I'm calling for Theo Drakos."

"Oh." The word was bright with surprise. "May I tell him who's calling?"

Fiona swallowed hard. “Yes. This is Fiona Western.”

“Just one moment. Theo, telephone!”

Fiona’s heart pounded as though it were trying to escape her rib cage. As the silence stretched, her nerves wound tighter. Why was it taking him so long to come to the phone?

Finally, there was a fumbling sound on the other end of the line, then Theo’s voice. “Hello?”

“Hi. It’s Fiona.” Fiona heard her relief and wondered if Theo did too. “It’s so good to hear your voice. I’ve been so worried.”

There was a pause. “You didn’t need to be worried.”

“Didn’t need to be worried? Theo Drakos, I came home from the beach and your house was gone! I couldn’t believe it.”

There was another lull on the line. Fiona’s insides felt as tightly twisted as the telephone cord. But maybe silences were normal on a long-distance call. Fiona had never made one before. How much would this cost? She’d have to pay back Mom and Dad.

“I’m sure others in town told you that Mom and I weren’t home when it happened.”

“Well, yeah.”

“So, then, you didn’t need to be worried.” The flatness in Theo’s voice felt like a slap. He didn’t even sound like her Theo.

"If the situation was reversed, and it was *you* coming home from vacation to find out that *my* house had burned down—"

"The situation never would've been reversed," Theo snapped. Now he *really* didn't sound like her Theo. "This never would've happened to someone like you."

Fiona could barely take a full breath. "Why are you acting like this?"

"I'm sorry you were scared." His voice was tight. Was he angry, or was he trying to hide his emotions? Both sounded the same with Theo. "I'm fine. Mom's fine. And I think that's all that really needs to be said on the matter. Goodbye, Fiona."

"Theo, wait!"

But the line was already dead.

She fumbled the receiver back into its cradle. What had just happened? He'd dismissed her concern—dismissed *her*—as though she didn't matter to him at all.

Frieda breezed into the room, fastening a large earring as she came through. "Have you seen my jellies? I thought they were—" She stopped as soon as she saw Fiona's face. "Did you call him?"

Fiona nodded. There was a large lump wedged in her throat, preventing her from speaking. She could tell her sister was looking at her, but nothing else, because her vision was too blurry.

"What happened?"

Fiona shook her head. She didn't really know the answer to the question, but she had to try. "I guess..." Fiona swallowed hard. "I guess he doesn't want to be friends anymore."

And then the lump in her throat was gone, and Fiona's tears flowed freely.

Hannah had never thrown a party in her apartment while the Hot Spot was open. She'd suspected she might come to regret this decision, but so far it had been easier than she'd expected. This was largely due to Jacob's capabilities in the kitchen, as well as her sister-in-law's presence upstairs. Whenever Hannah went down to the restaurant to see if Jacob needed help in the kitchen, or to grab party food she had stashed in the Hot Spot's refrigerator, Allison hopped into hostess mode and made sure everything was taken care of in Hannah's absence.

But even if the party *had* been more challenging to throw, the flush of delight on Aunt Fiona's cheeks as the room filled with all her friends from Blackberry Valley would've made the evening worth it. Aunt Fiona looked as though she was having the time of her life.

"Your aunt is a hoot," Elaine said as Hannah passed by the hostess stand on her way back upstairs. "I want to grow up to be just like her."

Hannah grinned. "Isn't she great? I think she has more energy in her fifties than I do in my thirties."

Elaine chuckled and then shifted her focus to the door as a family entered. Hannah jogged upstairs, where it was noticeably much warmer. She bumped on the air conditioner and increased the speed on the overhead fan.

"You're going to eat at some point, right?" Aunt Fiona asked, materializing at her side. With one hand she held a full plate and the other hand a glass, but she gave Hannah a kiss on the cheek all the same.

Hannah smiled. "At some point, yes. You're having fun?"

"This is the best birthday I've had in ages. Usually, because of my job, I go out for dinner with friends I've known for six months or less. And that's fun too, but there's just something about old friends." Her eyes caught on someone, and they sparkled. "Speaking of old friends, there's Rusty Studebaker." Aunt Fiona rushed to Rusty with wide open arms, the food on her plate sliding precariously. "So good to see you. And this is your wife?"

"Yes, this is Pamela." Rusty beamed at the woman beside him, who had curly dark hair and black-rimmed glasses that made her look like a very cool librarian.

"Wonderful to meet you." Aunt Fiona smiled at Pamela as though they were already good friends. "Your husband is the reason I passed my math classes and graduated from high school."

Pamela returned the smile. "He has a gift."

Rusty glanced behind him, then said to Aunt Fiona, "And I know it's been a while, but I think you know the friend we brought along too."

He stepped aside and gestured to the tall man on the stairs behind them.

"Hello, Fiona," he said.

The man had dark hair touched by gray at the temples, and a prominent nose that gave him a distinguished look, like a man in a classical painting. His mouth was curved in a slight smile, and Hannah was sure she'd never seen someone look as intensely at a person as he was looking at her aunt right now.

Aunt Fiona just stared back at the man, her mouth agape. The silence stretched so long that Hannah wondered if Aunt Fiona was going to reply at all.

But then she swallowed and inhaled shakily. "Hello, Theo. So good to see you."

Chapter Eleven

Hannah said it was open invitation," Rusty said, his eyes shifting between the two. "So I thought it'd be okay to invite Theo."

"Of course it's okay." Aunt Fiona's voice registered an octave higher than usual. "It's a surprise, but that's great. What's life without a few surprises, right?"

Theo's smile hung crooked. "You did always love surprises." He hadn't stepped across the threshold yet, like he wasn't totally sure it was okay to enter.

"Some surprises, yes." Aunt Fiona turned to Hannah. "This is my niece, Hannah. She's Frieda's oldest. Hannah, you know Rusty, of course, and his wife, Pamela. And this is Theo Drakos. He's... We used to be..."

Hannah stretched out her hand so Aunt Fiona wouldn't be burdened by having to label their relationship. "So good to meet you. I'm glad you could come." She appraised him. So this was Apollo.

Theo's hand enveloped hers. "Thank you for having me."

"This is Hannah's apartment." With her chin, Aunt Fiona gestured to the room, as though otherwise they might be confused by what she was referring to. "And the Hot Spot is her restaurant. Have you ever been?"

"It's one of my favorites." Pamela smiled at Hannah. "I love your fried chicken salad. And in the spring you had a potato leek soup that I still think about."

Hannah felt herself blush. "Thank you. That's so kind."

"I'm afraid I haven't had the pleasure yet," Theo said. "This is my first time back to Blackberry Valley in years."

His dark eyes slid back to Aunt Fiona, who looked away under the pretense of taking a sip from her drink.

"Where do you live now?" Hannah asked, spurred by a desire to be polite.

"Louisville."

"Great city. Have you lived there long?"

"Since college." Theo looked at Aunt Fiona, who still had her gaze averted, then turned back to Hannah. "I teach computer science at a high school there."

"College is where Theo and I reconnected." Rusty clapped a hand on Theo's shoulder. "We knew each other a bit in high school, but with everything that happened and him moving away—"

"You should all come in and get food," Aunt Fiona interrupted. Her voice still had that same strange, high tone. "Everything is delicious. I'll show you where the plates are."

Aunt Fiona spun away with such gusto that the contents of her own plate nearly slid off onto her white linen dress. She gave a nervous laugh. "Well, that could've been embarrassing."

Hannah smiled as Aunt Fiona led them away to the kitchen. She knew Aunt Fiona was currently uncomfortable, but hopefully once the initial shock wore off, the surprise of seeing Theo again would feel pleasant. Healing.

Her gaze trailed after them but then caught sight of her niece staring at a spilled soda with a look of horror on her sweet face.

Hannah rushed to Ava, whose cheeks were bright red. "No big deal, honey. I'll help you clean this up."

"I didn't mean to knock it over," Ava said, barely above a whisper.

"Of course you didn't. Accidents happen to all of us. We'll have this cleaned up in no time."

By the time Hannah and Ava finished cleaning up the spill, Ava was back to her usual cheerful self. Hannah assured her niece that it was fine to get herself a new soda—this appeared to have been Ava's biggest concern in knocking over the can—and then surveyed the party. Aunt Fiona and Theo stood in a clump with Rusty, Pamela, and several others who must be high school friends, based on their age. Aunt Fiona didn't look quite as flustered as she had a few minutes ago, though there did appear to be a careful gap between her and Theo.

They stood relatively close to where Hannah had discovered the letter and compass. If Theo was, indeed, the one who placed the items there, did he remember that he'd done so? Hannah hoped Aunt Fiona would ask him about it. She'd love to solve that mystery.

After another moment of hesitation, Hannah left the party and jogged down the stairs to check on the Hot Spot. Every table in the dining room was full, and several groups gathered in the waiting area, which likely meant Jacob was swamped in the kitchen. Sure enough, Hannah walked in to find Jacob managing multiple pans while simultaneously prepping ingredients.

"You should've called for me," Hannah said as she slipped into her chef's coat. After sending a quick text to Allison, asking her to keep an eye on food up there, Hannah took over dicing avocados.

"I thought I could handle it, but then about fifteen minutes ago it's as if everybody in town decided to show up and eat," Jacob called above the noise of the kitchen. "Thanks for coming down."

Hannah and Jacob had worked together long enough that she was able to see where she should step in. Within about twenty minutes, they were caught up on orders, and Jacob stopped clenching his teeth the way he often did when he was under stress.

As Raquel scooped several appetizers onto a tray, she called out, "Hannah? Your sister-in-law wanted to know if you have more fruit kebabs stashed anywhere."

"Yes, I have more down here. I'll take them up when I go."

Hannah spent a few more minutes prepping ingredients and cleaning the workspace as best she could before taking the refill of fruit upstairs. She found Allison wiping the counter clean of crumbs and spilled dipping sauces.

"My children," Allison said as an explanation, mouth quirked in an affectionate smile.

Hannah lifted the empty platter from the counter and replaced it with the new full one. "Thanks for letting me know we were low. How's everything else looking?"

"There are a few coming back for seconds, but most have moved on to desserts." Allison held the dishcloth under running water. She lowered her voice to a whisper and asked, "What's the deal with that tall guy next to Aunt Fiona? I'm getting 'high school sweetheart' vibes."

Hannah peeked to Allison's right. The group of Aunt Fiona's classmates had swelled, but she was now turned toward Theo. They spoke to each other, and both had pink cheeks and shy smiles. The coloring could also be due to the warmth of Hannah's apartment—her air conditioner was really struggling to keep up—but she didn't think that was entirely the reason.

Hannah raised her eyebrows at her sister-in-law and said in a low voice, "That's Theo. According to Aunt Fiona, they were good friends in high school, but the friendship ended awkwardly and abruptly."

Allison's auburn eyebrows arched. "They look way too uncomfortable to have simply been good friends."

Hannah grinned. "I'm just repeating what Aunt Fiona said."

She peeked inside the other chafing dishes and agreed with Allison's assessment, that since most people were done eating, the food levels were fine. The cookie table looked well stocked too and required only a bit of rearranging.

Hannah took a chocolate chip mint cookie for herself and then turned to Allison. "I need to head back downstairs to keep Jacob from being overwhelmed again, but let me know if you need me."

Allison nodded, and Hannah clattered down the staircase as she shoved the cookie into her mouth. She arrived in the kitchen just as two big orders came through. As she slipped into her chef's coat once more, Jacob looked at her with relief.

"The guests upstairs are mostly done eating, so I'll be in here with you for a while," Hannah assured him.

This was a good thing, because orders rolled in steadily for the next hour. By the time Hannah felt comfortable leaving the kitchen again, it was after nine o'clock. On her way upstairs, she passed Uncle Gordon, Maeve, Hunter, and their three kids tromping downstairs.

"Thanks so much for hosting, Hannah," Maeve said as she leaned in for a farewell hug.

"Sorry we didn't get to talk more." Hannah ruffled Paxton's dark hair, and he gave her a grin that showed off his missing tooth.

"I'm sure we'll see you soon," Uncle Gordon said as they continued heading downstairs. "If nothing else, we'll have a big family dinner before Fiona leaves town."

The only people remaining upstairs were Dad, Allison, and Aunt Fiona.

"Aunt Fiona!" Hannah scolded at the sight of her aunt doing dishes. "This is your birthday party. What are you doing?"

Aunt Fiona barely glanced up at her. "Dishes."

"Well, yes, I see that." Hannah attempted to nudge her aunt out of the way with her hip, but Aunt Fiona stood strong. "You shouldn't be doing your own birthday dishes."

"Don't bother," Allison called to Hannah as she unwrapped the vacuum cord.

Dad dumped a stack of paper plates into the trash. "We already tried."

"Your dad and Allison are taking care of everything else, and Gordon is helping Maeve and Hunter get the kids out to the car." Aunt Fiona gestured with a soapy hand to the work being done. "Why should I just sit around when there are dishes to be done?"

"Because it's your birthday."

"If it makes you feel better, you can take care of the chafing dishes and the extra food. I didn't know what to do with any of that." Aunt Fiona smiled at her. "Everything was wonderful, Hannah. Thank you for doing this for me."

"How did things go with Theo?" Hannah asked, hungry for details.

And for actual food. She hadn't eaten anything but that cookie tonight.

"Fine." Aunt Fiona's voice had become high-pitched again. "Everything was fine."

Hannah loaded up a plate for herself and considered how much to push her aunt for information. It was her birthday, after all. Pressing her for details she didn't want to share didn't seem very celebratory. "I didn't know he was coming, or I would've warned you."

"Oh, I know that, honey." Aunt Fiona scrubbed a pan with more vigor than necessary. "It was fine that he was here. It wasn't a big deal. Really."

Hannah didn't answer.

Aunt Fiona glanced at her and then ducked her head over the sink. "It really wasn't. Actually, it was good to see him after all these years."

Hannah filled a ramekin with blue cheese dipping sauce. "Perhaps a little strange too?"

"Well, yes. That too. He…" Aunt Fiona swallowed hard. "He asked about meeting up tomorrow night. For dinner. Here at the Hot Spot."

"What'd you say?"

Aunt Fiona looked at her, and Hannah worried that she had said no. "I said yes, but I'm not sure I should have." Aunt Fiona's focus returned to the pile of dirty dishes. "I don't know that it's a good idea."

"Why not?"

"Because we're not sixteen anymore. It's been forty years. In fact, with how long it's been since we last spoke, I could've turned sixteen two and a half more times."

Hannah watched as Aunt Fiona's scrubbing grew even more intense. She sensed that she shouldn't try to argue the validity of this point with her aunt, but rather let her talk. "That's true, I suppose."

"If Theo wanted to talk to me before now, he certainly could have," Aunt Fiona continued. "Sure, there was a period of time where it would've been difficult—though not impossible—for him to find me. But not for the last couple of decades. He even admitted he looked me up on social media. For years now, he's been a few clicks away from sending me a message and he *didn't*. He chose not to."

Hannah was very attached to the sheet pan that Aunt Fiona was scrubbing with such vigor, but she resisted the urge to remove the steel wool from her aunt's grasp. "Did he offer an explanation of why?"

Finally, Aunt Fiona ceased scrubbing. "He said he felt awkward."

When Aunt Fiona didn't continue, Hannah swallowed her bite and said, "That seems valid. A lot of time had passed."

"He said he felt terrible about how he treated me on the phone the last time we talked." Aunt Fiona's voice was soft, making it challenging for Hannah to hear above the whir of the vacuum on the other side of the apartment. "That his behavior wasn't about me."

"That must've been nice to hear."

Aunt Fiona's shoulders rose and lowered in a sharp shrug. "But it doesn't change what happened, does it? It doesn't change how he hurt me."

"Did you say that to him?"

"I wanted to, but then Texas showed up, and that was the end of our private conversation."

"I'm sorry, *who* showed up?"

"Texas," Aunt Fiona said, laughing. She paused rinsing and stared at the ceiling for a moment. "I honestly can't think of his real name right now. He moved here from Dallas in eighth grade, and Texas is what we always called him."

"I assume you didn't ask Theo about the compass or the note that I found?"

Aunt Fiona pulled the drain on the sink. "No, but I will tomorrow night."

"What time are you meeting for dinner?" Hannah asked. "I'll have Elaine save a table for you."

Hannah knew exactly which one she wanted to use too. The table for two with a view of Main Street, where she and Liam had spent so many enjoyable meals with each other.

"Six. Will you be there?" Aunt Fiona's eyes pleaded with Hannah.

"Yes, of course."

"Not that I'm afraid of spending time with Theo. It's just been a while."

"Long enough that you could've turned sixteen two and a half more times," Hannah said with a grin. "That's what I've been told."

Aunt Fiona scowled at her teasing, but the effect was dampened by the amused sparkle in her eyes.

"And you had *no* idea he was going to show up?" Lacy asked as she handed Hannah a plate holding a BLT sandwich. "Don't people RSVP anymore?"

Hannah gladly accepted the plate. "To be fair to Theo, I told Rusty that it was an open invitation and to invite anyone he thought would enjoy reconnecting with Aunt Fiona. But I didn't imagine it would be *Theo* showing up."

"I still think of him as Apollo." Lacy slowly lowered herself into a seat at the Minyards' kitchen table. "Did you talk to him about finding the compass and the letter?"

"Not yet, but Theo and Aunt Fiona are meeting for dinner at the Hot Spot, and she's going to ask him about them."

Lacy gasped. "Like a date?"

"That's not how my aunt would describe it. She would say that it's more like two estranged friends from high school getting together to catch up over a meal."

Lacy grinned. "Kinda sounds like a date. How'd your aunt seem?"

"More nervous than happy. And it's clear she feels hurt and angry about how things ended between them."

"Let's pray, and then I have questions." Lacy bowed her head and Hannah did the same. "Lord, thank You so much for Hannah and her friendship. Thank You for her willingness to help me out on the farm this morning, and thank You for this food. In Jesus's name, Amen."

"Amen," Hannah echoed.

Lacy passed Hannah a bag of potato chips. "So, the last time your aunt and Theo spoke before last night was a phone call in 1986?"

"That's what she told me." Hannah shook a few kettle chips onto her plate. "And she said he made it clear that he didn't want to talk to her anymore."

"Wow. Then I understand Fiona's conflicting emotions. A lot of time has passed."

Hannah took a large bite of her sandwich, which Lacy had insisted on as payment for Hannah coming over this morning to assist with a few chores. The sandwich was unnecessary, but delicious and appreciated. Neil was typically able to do the chores that were too difficult or dangerous for a woman who was eight months pregnant, but Saturday was a busy day at Legend & Key Bookstore, which meant he had to be at the store earlier than other days. While Hannah wouldn't want to be a farmer all the time, she enjoyed helping out occasionally.

And she should enjoy the quality time with Lacy while she could still get it.

Melancholy swelled inside Hannah. Why did she keep having thoughts like that when it was just the two of them? How ridiculous to spend her time with Lacy feeling sad that soon she wouldn't have *as* much time with her. Especially when she didn't even know if that was true.

Hannah pushed the feelings away. "They were really sweet together, and it was clear Theo came with the hope of making amends." She thought of the pretty flush on her aunt's cheeks. "I think Aunt Fiona will forgive him for what happened."

"Okay, good." Lacy crunched into a carrot stick. "Otherwise, she might never ask why the note and compass were left at the firehouse, and I'm so curious about that."

"Me too," Hannah said. "I wanted to ask last night, but it didn't seem like a very polite way to greet someone I had barely met."

"I wish you didn't care so much about being polite, because then I would know the answer."

Hannah was about to tease back, but the sudden grimace that appeared on Lacy's face stole the words. "Lacy, what's wrong?"

"I'm fine." Lacy's smile was strained, and her right hand splayed over her round belly. "It's just a contraction."

"A contraction?" Hannah yelped, jumping to her feet. "Are you in labor?"

Lacy shook her head. A moment later, she exhaled slowly. "They're Braxton Hicks contractions, not the real thing. Which is unfortunate, because they're uncomfortable."

Hannah put a hand over her racing heart. "You scared me."

"I see that." Lacy grinned up at her. "You can sit. You won't need to rush me to the hospital or anything."

Hannah sank into her seat. "How often does that happen?"

"Some days I don't have any that I notice. Other days, I have quite a few. That was my first one today." Lacy shrugged as if it was no big deal.

Maybe it wasn't. Hannah had no idea. She nibbled at her sandwich and tried to imagine what it would feel like to know she might give birth to a baby at any moment. To know she was on the cusp of everything changing.

"Are you scared?" Hannah asked.

"A little. Mostly about the pain. But there'll be a baby on the other side." Lacy smiled, soft and sweet. "That's pretty great to think about."

The fear Hannah had felt a moment ago ebbed. "It is. I can't wait to meet this little boy or girl."

Lacy grinned. "Just think. Next year at this time, I'll have a baby crawling around here. And you'll be a married woman."

"A lot of change is coming," Hannah said, trying to match Lacy's enthusiasm.

These were happy changes, but even so, Hannah couldn't fully ignore the unease that bubbled up whenever she thought of them.

Chapter Twelve

"This is so nice of you," Aunt Fiona said from the passenger seat. "I know your Saturdays must be really busy."

"No busier than any other day. And I'm glad to have the time with just you."

The sun burned through the window on Hannah's side of the car, and she adjusted the vent so that cool air blew directly on her face. After finishing lunch at Lacy's, Hannah had gone directly to her dad's house to pick up her aunt for an afternoon of shopping.

Aunt Fiona's gaze drifted off to the right. "Hannah, do you mind if we take a brief detour to Lake Blackberry? I haven't been out there in ages, and I hear it's changed a lot."

Hannah let her foot off the gas. "Sure. I don't remember the last time I was out there myself. Liam and I considered the clubhouse for our wedding reception, but then I called and found out how much it was to rent."

Aunt Fiona smiled, seeming amused. "When your mom and I were kids, Lake Blackberry was practically a pond. Maybe there were a few people who went out there to fish, but it wasn't anything special or pretty. That didn't happen until I was in college."

Sensing her aunt had more to say, Hannah held her tongue.

Aunt Fiona fussed with the hem of her summer dress. "I still think about it sometimes, driving out here that day with Frieda after we got home from vacation. I had a bag of saltwater taffy in my lap, and I was teasing your mom because she thought Gabriel Prentiss *maybe* liked her." The wistful smile died on Aunt Fiona's face. "And then to arrive at Theo's and see the house was gone. To have no idea what had happened to him—" She bit off the words, pressing her lips together tightly.

"I can't imagine how awful that was for you."

"I'm having a hard time not feeling angry with him, even all these years later," Aunt Fiona admitted. Her fingers tangled in her necklace and twisted. "Not for the fire of course, or even for his leaving town without saying anything to me. It wasn't so easy to stay in contact with someone back then. But the way he spoke to me on the phone when I called him—I'm having trouble getting past that." Aunt Fiona's jaw set. The call may have happened forty years ago, but the pain hadn't gone away.

Hannah wished she could hug her aunt, but it was impossible while she was driving. "I'm praying that dinner tonight is a good thing," Hannah said. "That it'll bring about healing for you both."

"I hope so," Aunt Fiona murmured.

Moments later, Hannah's Subaru crested the hill, and below they could see the sun glinting off the pear-shaped lake surrounded by large houses.

"I always thought this view was beautiful," Aunt Fiona said. "Especially back when the land was wooded."

"There are a decent number of mature trees around the clubhouse and the park, but they must've taken out a bunch when they put in the neighborhood. Do you want me to drive the perimeter road?"

Aunt Fiona waved a dismissive hand. "We don't need to do the whole Blackbird Road loop. That would take too much time. Mostly

I just want to see what replaced Theo's house, and I think I can already see it. He lived on this side of the lake."

While Hannah had never been one to be awed by big houses, she could understand the appeal of living on Lake Blackberry. The houses were beautifully maintained, distinct from one another, and each lot looked to be half an acre, so there was space for privacy within the community. Most of the houses had small docks in the backyards. Hannah imagined it would be lovely to drink her morning coffee on a patio overlooking the lake.

"This was Theo's," Aunt Fiona murmured as they approached the first house. "You'd never know it now, because it was a gravel driveway and a tiny ranch with peeling paint. I think their entire house was the size of this family's garage."

Hannah assessed the brick home. Or was it technically a mansion? The beautiful house sat on a wide, manicured yard, and had a wraparound porch and three-car garage. One of the garage doors was open, showcasing a canary-yellow Jeep Wrangler. The sight made her frown. Hadn't she seen that Jeep recently? Who did that belong to?

"You can turn around anytime," Aunt Fiona said. "That's all I wanted to see. I wonder if Theo has been out here yet. So much has changed."

Hannah pulled into the next driveway to turn her car around. "I'm learning that change makes me very nervous."

Aunt Fiona huffed a tiny laugh. "I think that makes you normal. Change is scary for everyone."

"Not you," Hannah said. "You seem to embrace change, with how often you move and make new friends."

Aunt Fiona frowned. "I don't think I'd go so far as to say I *embrace* change. But I don't fear it like I once did."

"Why do you think that is?"

Her aunt's frown deepened. "I suppose I have learned to lean on the unchanging nature of God. My life is nothing like I thought it would be when I was a kid, but the Lord's faithfulness has been abundant through it all. I know that I can trust Him with my path, regardless of where the road leads or how life shifts."

Hannah's eyes burned with unshed tears. "That's beautiful. And I know all that, but I wish I *felt* it more in my heart, you know?"

"I definitely know. It didn't come naturally to me." Aunt Fiona gave a humorless laugh. "That trust came from routinely being knocked off the path I thought I was supposed to be on, only to have the Lord lovingly lift me up and set me on my feet again. He's been so good to me."

Hannah considered how it felt to be knocked off paths as she navigated back onto the main road. "You know, I don't think I find that very comforting, Aunt Fiona."

Aunt Fiona chuckled. "No, I understand that. But often the best things in life come just on the other side of pain or discomfort. You know that as well as I do."

She certainly did. And she really didn't like it.

Hannah found it challenging to keep her eyes off Aunt Fiona and Theo's table. Five minutes ago she'd sent Raquel out with a complimentary spinach dip appetizer, but her aunt and Theo were so deeply engaged in conversation that they hadn't touched it. Hannah wanted to ask Raquel if she'd overheard any of their conversation, but Aunt Fiona deserved privacy. Whatever details she wanted Hannah to know, she would share later.

Hannah resolved to focus on takeout orders, but still her gaze drifted their direction way more than it should have. Aunt Fiona and Theo were finally eating the spinach dip, so that was something. A few minutes later, she peeked again. To her surprise, Aunt Fiona was waving Hannah over to the table.

She set aside the rolls of receipt tape she'd been restocking—a task that was entirely an excuse to stay in the dining room longer—and hurried to their table. Even though Aunt Fiona had been adamant that this wasn't a date, just two old friends catching up with each other, both of them looked as though they'd taken extra care with their appearance.

Well, it was hard for her to judge with Theo, since this was only the second time she had seen him, and both times she assumed he'd dressed carefully. But Hannah knew her aunt, and she'd definitely made a special effort. Aunt Fiona's blond hair wasn't in its usual ponytail, and she wore a summery pink dress that she'd bought that afternoon while they were shopping.

"How is everything?" Hannah asked as she came alongside their table. "Is there anything else I can get you?"

"Actually, I was telling Theo about what you found in your apartment." Aunt Fiona fiddled with one of her silver hoop earrings. "When you get a moment, would you mind bringing down the compass and the note?"

Upon seeing the anticipatory expression on Theo's face, delight surged through Hannah. "Of course. I'll be right back."

She hurried up to her apartment. When she returned to the dining room holding the compass and note, Aunt Fiona scooted over in the booth to make room for her.

"Do you have a few minutes to sit with us?"

"I do." Hannah took the offered seat and placed Theo's compass and the note in front of him. With a smile, she said, "I'm so glad I can return these to you."

Theo stared at the two items, then slowly reached out and lifted the compass with his right hand, then the note with his left. When he looked at Hannah, his eyes brimmed with tears. "Thank you."

Hannah nodded, feeling her own eyes burn.

"Theo?" Aunt Fiona spoke his name in a gentle voice that she probably used when speaking to patients. "Why did you hide these in the firehouse?"

Theo ran a thumb over the face of the compass with a sad smile. "They were the only things I had left after the fire. Both were in my pocket when it happened."

"Will you tell us what happened that night?" Aunt Fiona asked.

Theo didn't speak, just continued gazing at the relics from his teenage years.

"I can leave, if you'd like," Hannah offered, scooting to exit the booth.

Theo smiled at her. "No, please stay. I really appreciate you finding these. You have no idea what it means to me to have them back." His gaze shifted to Aunt Fiona. "I made so many mistakes. I'm sorry, Fiona."

"We were sixteen. It's understandable." Aunt Fiona had softened since the conversation last night, as Hannah had assumed she would.

"Everything changed so fast," Theo murmured. "I didn't know how to handle it. One moment, I was eating grilled hot dogs—" He grinned at Aunt Fiona. "Remember how the fire department always grilled hot dogs for the Fourth of July?"

Aunt Fiona gave a happy groan. "Those were the best."

"I don't know why, but they really were. Mom said she felt like she was getting away with something, not having to make dinner. She made a dessert to add to the potluck, of course, but being off the hook for a meal probably felt amazing as a single parent. But one minute, I was hanging out with friends, happy and carefree and eating hot dogs. The next, Kenneth Cutuli was there, telling me they'd had a call at the station and our house was on fire. We found Mom and got out there as soon as we could, but the house was already gone by then. It burned so fast."

"I hate that I wasn't there for you." Aunt Fiona's voice was watery. "I can't even imagine how awful that experience was for you and Ivy."

Theo frowned. "I'd always taken care of my mom, but that night I failed her."

"You didn't," Hannah said at the same Aunt Fiona said, "It wasn't your fault."

Theo's smile was tight. "Thanks, ladies, but I disagree. Typically, I was good at going through the house before we left and making sure all the candles were blown out and the burners were off. Especially if Mom had been in the kitchen, which she had been. She'd made an apple pie to take to the potluck. I still remember how the whole house smelled of cinnamon and apples." He grimaced. "I haven't had an appetite for apple pie ever since. I've never forgiven myself for being distracted that night."

"You were sixteen," Aunt Fiona reminded him. "Making sure the oven is off because your mom baked isn't something a sixteen-year-old should have to do."

Theo shrugged. "Even so." Clearly, he was unwilling to let himself off the hook.

"Accidents like that happen," Hannah said. "That doesn't make it your fault."

Aunt Fiona sat up straighter. "And we don't even know that the oven being left on is what caused the fire. I always heard it could've been fireworks that were shot off near your house."

Theo wore a skeptical expression. "I don't know about that. Mom sure thought it was her fault. She said she'd probably left something on when she was making the pie or curling her hair. I overheard her talking to Kenneth's wife, Joan, that night. The Cutulis took us in, of course. They were the best."

"But Ivy *thinking* it was her fault doesn't mean that it actually was," Aunt Fiona insisted. "There's no way to know."

"No, but Mom was confident enough that she told our landlord that was what happened. He was great about it. He told her that others had seen fireworks being shot off on the vacant lot next door, and that so far as he—and the insurance company—were concerned, *that* was the cause of the fire. That those unknown people were responsible. Mom always thought he made all that up."

"If he did make up that story, it was generous of him," Aunt Fiona said.

"Surprisingly generous, really," Theo agreed. "He hadn't been a very pleasant landlord up until then, but I'm grateful that Lawrence showed kindness to us in that moment. As it is, Mom still shuts down all attempts to talk about the fire. I know she blames herself."

A silence fell over the table. Hannah nodded to the note and compass. "If you were staying at Kenneth's place, how did those end up at the firehouse?"

"The morning Mom and I were leaving for my relatives' house in Lexington, Kenneth was on duty. I came here to say goodbye to him, but he was out on a call, so I waited upstairs." Theo pushed a hand through his thick hair, his cheeks were a touch pink. "I loved living here. I was distraught over having to leave, and I decided it would be less painful if I cut all ties with Blackberry Valley. Yet the idea of throwing away my compass, or my letter from you, Fiona, was unbearable. So I hid them instead. I knew if I changed my mind, I could ask Kenneth or one of the Wayfinders to retrieve them for me."

Aunt Fiona wrapped her lightweight cardigan tighter around her body. "The compass I understand, but why did you have my note with you?"

Theo's cheeks turned even redder. He looked out the window and said, "Because I carried it around with me all that summer."

"Oh." Aunt Fiona's eyes gleamed. "That's nice."

Theo scoffed. "Or pathetic."

Aunt Fiona beamed at him. "I don't think it's pathetic."

"I wish I could've known you both in high school," Hannah said. "My nickname probably would've been 'Banana' because Hannah Banana is about the only nickname I've ever had."

Theo chuckled. "I can't remember who started the nicknames. I think it was me?"

"No, it was me. I called you Apollo, and so you had to come up with a nickname for me."

"I did not *have* to come up with a nickname for you, thank you very much," Theo said. "I chose to. And Sunflower suited you because of your blond hair and sunny disposition."

Aunt Fiona snorted a laugh. "When we first met, I did *not* have a sunny disposition."

Theo smiled at Aunt Fiona with such affection, Hannah wanted to hug him. "But your sunny personality was there all along. It just needed a little coaxing to come forth."

"I can't even imagine my aunt being shy," Hannah said. "My whole life, she's been this vibrant, energetic person."

Aunt Fiona scraped up the last of the spinach dip. "Theo taught me to not be afraid."

"That's overselling what I did."

Aunt Fiona looked steadily at him. "No, it's not."

Theo flinched. "And then I taught you that I was a jerk. I still can't believe how I treated you on the phone that day."

She shook her head. "Please don't dwell on that anymore. I know we didn't feel like children at the time, but you *were* a child, and you were scared."

"Even though I was awful to you, it still meant so much to me that you'd gone to the effort to track down my aunt and uncle's phone number. I knew how hard that must have been for you." Theo reached a tentative hand across the table to Aunt Fiona. "I'm sorry that I wasn't a better friend to you."

Aunt Fiona reached back and clasped Theo's hand. "I'm just glad we're here now."

Hannah took this as her cue to excuse herself. She stood, gathering the empty spinach dip bowl. "I'll get these out of your way. I imagine Jacob needs my help in the kitchen, and your entrees should be out any minute."

Hannah wasn't even sure they'd heard her, but then Theo called out, "Hannah?"

She turned and found him smiling at her.

"Thank you," he said, "for finding what I lost and returning it to me."

She was fairly sure that he wasn't talking about just the compass and note.

Chapter Thirteen

Typically, Sundays were a much-needed day of rest for Hannah, but today the Hot Spot had been rented out for a one-hundredth birthday party celebration. She and Jacob worked side-by-side before the party to prepare food, and when guests began to trickle in, Hannah moved out to the dining room to help Raquel take drink orders. The family had brought bunches of balloons for the tables, as well as framed pictures of the birthday girl from her youth, and the restaurant bubbled with energy.

"I love when we have parties," Raquel said as they stood at the soda fountain together. "There's something really fun about all the people in the dining room knowing one another. It creates a different energy in the room."

Hannah looked over her shoulder and grinned at the sight of the guests dragging tables into clumps or crossing the room to hug someone seated in a booth. "You're right. It *is* nice."

"And I hope I look that good when I'm a hundred," Raquel added.

Hannah glanced back at the guest of honor, with her wide smile and sparkling blue eyes. "Isn't that the truth?"

"I asked what her secret is." Raquel lowered her voice to a conspiratorial whisper. "She said daily naps and dark chocolate."

Hannah snorted with laughter. "That's a health regimen I can get behind."

"Right?" Raquel arranged glasses on her tray. "I think this is all I can manage. I'll come back for the others."

Hannah continued to fill drink orders. The friendly chatter in the full dining room made happiness sweep through her soul. She'd also had a whole hour for a video chat with Liam after church. Seeing his face and having an extended time to talk had buoyed her spirits, though she wished he had a clearer idea of when he would be able to come home.

Raquel finished distributing drinks, and the two of them stood at the edge of the party, keeping an eye on the buffet line as guests made their way through. This part of celebrations at the Hot Spot, where she just stood around and kept an eye on things, always made Hannah feel antsy, even though she knew there was nothing else to be done except be available in case a guest needed something.

"Do you have anything fun planned for tonight?" Hannah asked.

Raquel nodded, and her dark curls bounced. "Marshall and I are seeing a movie. Even simple dates feel wonderful after he was in Chicago all that time."

"I can imagine," Hannah said, wondering what Liam was doing right now. "It's hard to be apart from each other. And Liam won't be gone nearly as long as Marshall was."

Raquel gave her a sympathetic face. "Any word on when he'll be home?"

"Not yet. Hopefully soon."

"I hope so. Oh!" Raquel bounced on her heels. "And if there's time tonight, I'll be doing laundry."

Hannah would've thought Raquel's enthusiasm was sarcastic except that a genuine smile stretched across her face.

"Wow," Hannah said. "I need to do laundry too, but you look way happier about it than I feel."

"That's because Lawrence Underhill Properties replaced the washers and dryers in each apartment. I'd complained multiple times that my dryer didn't work properly, and this new manager finally paid attention and replaced them. You met her earlier in the week. Remember Courtney?"

"Yes, she seemed lovely," Hannah said, but she was distracted, thinking about what Theo had said yesterday. Hadn't he said the landlord's name was Lawrence?

As the connection clicked into place, Hannah felt the same satisfaction as when all the ingredients came together for a fantastic new recipe. The Lawrence who had rented the house to Theo and his mom was surely the same as the founder of Lawrence Underhill Properties.

How had Theo described the landlord's reaction to the fire? *Surprisingly generous.* Theo had even said that Lawrence hadn't been a pleasant landlord up until then, which coincided with stories she'd heard from Raquel. Now that Hannah suspected Theo's former landlord was the same grumpy man who'd accused his daughter of excessive spending when she made changes that sounded necessary, Hannah also thought it seemed "surprisingly generous" that Lawrence had been so forgiving when one of his rental properties burned to the ground. Especially considering the possibility that it was the result of a tenant's mistake. Why would he have done that?

"You have extra corn salad ready, right?"

Hannah blinked back into focus and instantly noticed why Raquel was asking. The salad barely covered the bottom of the serving bowl. "Yes, thank you. I'll refill it."

She rushed to the kitchen to get the extra batch of corn salad they'd made.

"Hey, boss," Jacob greeted her through a cloud of steam created by the boiled potatoes. "The potato salad reminded me of a restaurant I went to a few years ago in Oklahoma where the menu was entirely baked potatoes. Ham and cheese baked potatoes, Philly cheesesteak baked potatoes, BLT baked potatoes. You name it, they put it on a potato. What do you think of a special section in our fall or winter menu for loaded baked potatoes?"

Hannah opened her mouth to remind Jacob what she often did—that a restaurant had to be *profitable* in addition to having a creative menu—but she closed her mouth. She'd just been thinking about miserly Lawrence Underhill, and even though the profitability of the Hot Spot was a high priority, the idea of shooting down Jacob's idea for that reason alone didn't sit well with her.

"So long as we use ingredients on the baked potatoes that are also used in other seasonal dishes, I think that could be a nice addition to the menu, Jacob."

Her chef beamed in response.

After an hour of scrolling the internet, Hannah gave up on finding additional information about the fire that had taken Theo's house, or confirming whether Lawrence Underhill had been the landlord. *The Blackberry Valley Chronicle* didn't have an online archive dating back that far, and there were no relevant hits for internet searches like *Blackberry Valley fire July 4, 1986.*

Hannah glanced at the time. Her staff would arrive soon. She was about to close her computer when she thought to run one more search for *Lawrence Underhill Properties Blackberry Valley.*

The company website was beautiful and sleek, with a slideshow of buildings all over the county. Hannah clicked on the *About Us* page and skimmed through details of Lawrence's rags-to-riches story—from growing up in a shabby rented house, to now owning real estate all over the county and passing along the business to the next generation. Hannah frowned at the story. Somehow that made it worse that he'd generally been an uncaring landlord. He should've known better, having experienced such practices himself.

Alongside the text was a posed photo of Lawrence, Courtney, and Lincoln engrossed in some sort of discussion. The three of them were arranged in such a way that Lawrence appeared to be the wise business owner and Courtney and Lincoln were the eager pupils.

There wasn't anything *wrong* with the information on the website, but it still didn't sit right with Hannah. Everything was a little too picture-perfect.

As her staff arrived and they got to work preparing for Tuesday evening guests, Hannah's mind kept turning back to the conversation she'd overheard between Lawrence, Courtney, and Lincoln. Maybe that was why the website bothered her, because it didn't represent the behavior she'd seen when there wasn't a camera around.

But of course, that was *one* conversation. Maybe arguments among the three of them were unusual.

She needed to stop thinking about this. The dining room was nearly full by now, and Hannah had to-go orders that needed to be packed up.

"There's my lovely niece."

Hannah turned and grinned at her aunt, who stood on the other side of the counter. "And there's my lovely aunt. How are you?"

Hannah always thought her aunt was beautiful, but tonight she looked especially nice in a yellow floral sundress and dangling earrings.

"Very good. I'm picking up dinner to take to Rusty and Pamela's."

"That's interesting." Hannah peered inside the bag. "There are four meals on the receipt, not three. Did we make a mistake?"

Aunt Fiona blushed. "Theo will be there too."

"How surprising." Hannah used a voice that said she wasn't surprised at all. "He's staying in town for kind of a long time, isn't he?"

Aunt Fiona took the bag. "He's a teacher on summer break and enjoying some time with his friends, who he hasn't seen in a long time."

Hannah grinned. "How nice."

Aunt Fiona sighed, but she was smiling too. "Don't read too much into this, Hannah. Neither of us are who we were in high school, and there's no need to jump to conclusions about what it does or doesn't mean."

"I didn't jump to any conclusions," Hannah said, raising her hands. "All I said was that I didn't realize he was going to be in town so long."

Aunt Fiona fiddled with an earring as she bit her bottom lip.

Hannah hadn't intended for her teasing to make her aunt uncomfortable, so she quickly added, "You know what's interesting? I'm pretty sure I met his former landlord last week. Or I didn't *meet* him exactly, but he dined here, and it was memorable."

Aunt Fiona stopped fidgeting. "How so?"

Hannah explained what she'd overheard between Lawrence and his daughter, as well as her conversation with Lincoln afterward.

"Maybe there are two Lawrences managing rental properties," Hannah said. "But that seems unlikely to me."

"Me too," Aunt Fiona murmured. "I can ask Theo if he remembers. If he doesn't, he can ask Ivy for the landlord's full name."

"I didn't think much about it until Sunday when I was talking to one of my servers. Raquel rents an apartment from Lawrence Underhill Properties, and she's been delighted by the changes that have occurred since Courtney took over for her father. Raquel says it used to be that complaints from residents were ignored, but Courtney seems to be taking a different, more proactive approach and is investing in the properties they own."

"I wonder what Theo would have to say about that," Aunt Fiona said. "We were teenagers, so I never gave much thought to their renting the house rather than owning it, or what their landlord might've been like. I don't remember Theo saying anything about trouble with him back in the day either. Theo's comment about their landlord not being very pleasant was the first I'd ever heard about those problems."

Hannah packed several napkins in the to-go bag and handed it to her aunt. "If it's the same man, then it seems like Theo's surprise about Lawrence being generous with his mom was a legitimate thing to be surprised by. My limited exposure to Lawrence Underhill tells me he would've typically been unforgiving in a situation like that."

Aunt Fiona took the paper bag as she nodded. "And if Theo's right and Lawrence *was* behaving out of character, the question I'd like an answer to is why?"

The Hot Spot remained steadily busy that night, and Hannah bounced between helping Jacob in the kitchen and keeping to-go orders on track. A thrill of delight ran through her when she saw an order come in from the firehouse, but she promptly remembered that Liam wouldn't be the one picking it up.

Even though the restaurant was nearly full, Hannah felt loneliness sharp in her ribs. She ducked into her office, pulled out her phone, and typed, I MISS YOU. PLEASE SAY YOU'RE COMING HOME SOON.

Liam's reply came seconds later. I MISS YOU TOO. I'M HOPEFUL IT WON'T BE TOO MUCH LONGER. MAYBE ANOTHER WEEK?

Another week? She allowed herself a few minutes to feel how deeply she longed for Liam to be back home, then she put her phone away and returned to work. She did a quick survey of the dining room. There were a number of faces she recognized, including Connie Sanchez and her husband. They were seated beside the staff of *The Blackberry Valley Chronicle*, Jack Delaney, Pippa Nelson, and Marshall Fredericks, Raquel's boyfriend.

At the booth beside the newspaper staff sat Lincoln, having dinner with his older brother, Edward. Both men must've come to the restaurant straight from work, because Edward was still in his suit—though his jacket was off and his tie loosened—and Lincoln in a striped polo.

This was a nice-size crowd, especially for a Tuesday.

"Hey, boss, the ice maker is jammed," her waiter, Dylan Bowman, called to her. "Or broken. One of the two."

Hannah groaned under her breath. Hopefully it was a simple fix. The ice maker going out in the middle of summer would be a nightmare.

"Okay, thank you!" she called back with feigned cheeriness.

Hannah surveyed the ice maker, which *did* appear to be jammed rather than broken. What a relief. So long as she didn't break it in her efforts to dislodge the ice, they'd be fine.

As Hannah used a dinner knife to poke about the chute, she noticed Colt Walker, the youngest fireman at the station, chatting away with the Lake brothers like they were best buddies. Hannah hadn't realized they knew each other, but the more she thought about it, the less this surprised her. Edward and Lincoln had deep roots in Blackberry Valley, and Colt was a friendly fellow.

"Finally," Hannah said with a sigh of relief as the problematic ice chunk broke free and shattered on the floor. Having ice shards everywhere wasn't ideal, but it was a mess that could be cleaned up.

Raquel approached with several cups. "Working again?"

Hannah stepped aside and gestured to the machine. "Give it a try."

The ice flowed freely, and after exchanging a celebratory smile with Raquel, Hannah bent to collect the ice that had fallen to the ground before it became a slippery puddle.

She'd just dumped the ice in the sink when Colt greeted her with his usual amicable tone. "Hello there, Hannah. How are you?"

She smiled at him. Not only was he endlessly polite, but he also nearly always had a smile on his face. "I'm doing pretty well. You here to pick up that order?"

"Yes, ma'am."

"It should be ready. How are you doing?" Hannah led him to the shelf of to-go orders.

"Not bad. It's a bit odd at the firehouse with both Liam and Archer absent, but we're doing okay," Colt said. "Which reminds me—"

"Hannah, wait!"

She whirled toward Dylan's panicked voice and found him rushing forward with a credit card outstretched. "The men at Table Three say this is for the firemen's dinners."

Hannah took the card from Dylan and looked beyond him to confirm her recollection. Table Three was the Lake brothers.

Colt didn't seem startled by this turn of events. He waved and called out, "It's not necessary, but thank you."

Lincoln gave a single wave of his hand, both acknowledging and dismissing Colt's protest.

"Well, that's very kind," Hannah said. "Thanks, Dylan. I'll return the card once I'm done."

Dylan scampered back to his duties, and Hannah pulled up the order from the firehouse to run Lincoln's card.

Colt leaned against the counter. "They're big supporters of the fire department. If we're eating somewhere in uniform, and either of the Lake brothers are at the restaurant too, they'll often send over appetizers or buy our dinners." He shrugged. "It's a job perk."

"It's a well-deserved one. Although I guess I'm biased now that I'm engaged to a fireman." Hannah double-checked the to-go bag before passing it across the counter to Colt. "Were you going to tell me something before Dylan brought over the credit card?"

Colt's face was momentarily blank and then his eyes lit with remembrance. "Yes, thank you. Liam asked me to look up an old fire for you. I ran a search in the database, but we haven't migrated those records yet. I'm hoping to check the physical archives in the next day or two."

If Colt was curious about why Hannah wanted to see fire records from 1986, he didn't say so. Hannah considered explaining herself, and she would have if she was looking into the fire for personal reasons. But considering this was more about Theo than it was her, she decided to forgo volunteering details.

"Thank you so much for doing that, Colt. I know it has to be extra busy at the firehouse with two gone for the foreseeable future."

"It's no problem, Hannah."

Colt took the bag of food, and with one more wave and a "Thank you!" directed at the Lake brothers, he strode through the door.

Hannah carried the credit card back to the table and set it beside Lincoln's plate of smoked fried chicken. "That was very kind of you."

Lincoln shrugged as he returned the card to his wallet. "Nobody is more deserving than firemen, in my opinion. Those guys are heroes. You know my brother, Edward?"

Hannah turned and acknowledged Edward with a smile. "Yes, good to see you again, Edward."

Even with his jacket off and his tie loosened, Edward had a sleek, put-together look about him. He smiled at Hannah as he firmly grasped and shook her hand. "You're the owner, right? Hannah..."

"Prentiss," she supplied. "And yes, I am."

"Fine establishment you have here," Edward said as he gazed around the room. "And please give my compliments to your chef. This is one of the best Reuben sandwiches I've had in a long time."

Hannah had already noticed that Edward's plate was nearly clean.

"Oh, I completely agree. We make our dressing in-house, and that makes all the difference." She shifted her smile from Edward to Lincoln. "I'll let the two of you enjoy the rest of your meal, but I wanted to say thank you. My fiancé is Chief Berthold, so I also feel strongly about honoring our firemen."

"The Hot Spot does that well." Lincoln gestured around the restaurant, which, in addition to being housed in the original firehouse, also showcased the history of the Blackberry Valley Fire Department on its walls. "I especially like that picture over there, with Kenneth Cutuli. Do you remember me telling you about him last week? The fireman who led Wayfinders?"

"I do." Hannah turned in the direction Lincoln gestured. It was a photograph of the fire department from the late eighties, when Liam's dad had been fire chief. "I didn't realize Kenneth was in that picture. Will you point him out to me?"

Lincoln led her across the restaurant to the photo. "This is Kenneth." He pointed to a redheaded man with a large grin, an impressive mustache, and eyes shaped like crescents. "Kindest man I ever knew. He's the reason I wanted to be a fireman."

Hannah opened her mouth to ask why he wasn't a fireman but realized it could be a touchy subject and decided not to ask.

Lincoln must have noticed. "You might observe that I'm not a fireman. I volunteered at the department in high school, and it was clear to me that as much as I loved the *idea* of it, I don't have what it takes to be a good fireman." A look passed over his face that she couldn't easily name. Something akin to regret.

Hannah smiled, hoping to set him at ease. "Life doesn't always work out the way we expect, does it?"

Lincoln chuckled. "Certainly not. Especially when we're talking about the adults we dreamed we'd be when we were teenagers." He looked back at the picture. "Maybe if things had gone a little differently..." Again, that same expression took over his face. "No use dwelling on regrets now, I suppose. What's done is done."

Whatever he was referring to, he clearly felt remorseful. Hannah wanted to say something comforting, but didn't know what. Instead, she had Dylan take free desserts out to him and Edward. It wouldn't fix whatever had made Lincoln so sad, but it wouldn't hurt either.

Chapter Fourteen

As Wednesday evening stretched on, Hannah was delighted to see the largest table at the Hot Spot begin to fill up. Aunt Fiona had texted Hannah that afternoon to ask if she minded reserving the table for a last-minute Wayfinders reunion, which she'd been happy to do. The group began as Rusty, Theo, and Aunt Fiona, but gradually more Wayfinders trickled in until there were nine in total, including Edward and Lincoln. Laughter was plentiful as the group reminisced about hikes they'd taken, overnight backpacking trips that had gone awry, and funny things Kenneth had said.

While she'd never met Kenneth Cutuli, Hannah wished he was here now to see this. How remarkable that so many years later, the investment he made in a group of young men was still so visible.

At seven o'clock, when Hannah took over the hostess stand so Elaine could go on break, Aunt Fiona got up from the Wayfinders table and joined her. "Mind if I hang out with you for a bit?"

"Of course not. Are they getting too rowdy over there?" Hannah asked with a wink.

"I just wanted to give the guys some time on their own. I knew all of them in high school, but it's not like I was one of them."

Another roar of laughter rose up from the table.

Aunt Fiona shook her head with affection. "It's like they're teenagers again."

"It's sweet," Hannah said. She'd had plenty of friends in high school, but she didn't feel a particular bond with anyone from those days, other than Lacy.

Aunt Fiona turned back to Hannah, her expression serious. "Theo did confirm that Lawrence Underhill was the landlord. I asked him when he and I drove out to Lake Blackberry today."

"How did that go?"

"Not bad, actually." Aunt Fiona shrugged. "Theo said it was easier than he expected. He thought it was helpful that nothing looked like it used to, because that way it didn't *feel* like the same place where this tragic thing happened to him."

Hannah considered this. "I'm glad seeing the place again wasn't too painful."

"There's a lovely walking trail out there. It seems like a very nice place to live. My friend Jennifer and her husband love living out there. Of course, I could never afford a place like that."

Raquel and Dylan emerged from the kitchen with full trays, and Hannah nodded in their direction. "I think those are your entrees coming out."

"Then I'd better get back." Aunt Fiona reached out and squeezed Hannah's arm. "Would you like to come paddleboarding with Theo and me tomorrow? We saw some people doing that today on the lake and thought it looked like fun. There's a place to rent boards right there at the clubhouse."

"Paddleboarding on Lake Blackberry?" Hannah tried not to grin and failed. "That sounds an awful lot like a date."

Aunt Fiona rolled her eyes. "It's *not* a date because we're inviting your dad and Gordon, Drew's family, Gordon's family, and you."

"Well, in that case, then sure. I'd love to come with you."

"Great." Aunt Fiona beamed at her and took several steps back toward the table. "It's supposed to rain tomorrow morning, so we think arriving at the clubhouse around one would be best. Does that work for you?"

Hannah considered this. Starting at one meant she wouldn't be at the restaurant in time to help with prep, but she could be there by the opening. "Yes, that works for me, as long as I'm back before four."

"Great. Do you want us to pick you up or meet you at the clubhouse?"

"Let's meet at the clubhouse," Hannah said. "That way I can leave when I need to without inconveniencing anyone."

Aunt Fiona gave her a thumbs-up and returned to her table. Hannah's eyes lingered on the group for a moment, but Raquel and Dylan appeared to be doing a wonderful job taking care of the guests.

The main door opened and Hannah turned to find Colt had arrived, smiling as always.

Hannah grinned at him. "Did they send you to pick up the to-go order two nights in a row?"

Colt shrugged. "Just part of being the rookie, I guess. Doesn't bother me. I like the chance to get some fresh air."

"Come with me. I know your order was about ready a few minutes ago."

He followed Hannah to the counter, where she scanned the receipt and realized that everything was accounted for except for the four lemonades.

"Sorry about that," Hannah said. "These will just take a minute."

Colt trailed Hannah to the drink station. "No problem. Also, that fire you asked about? I have an update for you. Well, kind of. You said 1986, right?"

Hannah grabbed four to-go cups. "Yes, what'd you learn?"

His smile became apologetic. "It's nothing too exciting. I went to the archive room and—"

Edward materialized at the counter, a ketchup bottle in hand. "Hannah, any chance you have a replacement back there? This one is empty."

"No problem." Hannah walked the few feet to where the extra bottles were stored, grabbed a new one, and held it out to Edward. "I'll trade you. Is everything else okay?"

He flashed her a smile of white teeth. "Everything is great, as always. Thanks."

Edward turned on his heel, and Hannah fixed her attention on Colt once more. "So, what'd you learn about the fire?"

Colt had been fidgeting with a loose string on his cuff and finally tugged it free. "The fire you asked about was Fourth of July, 1986, right?"

"Yeah, that's the one."

Hannah realized Edward had ceased walking back to the table and was now standing a few feet away, smiling apologetically. "Sorry, but could I get an extra fork? I just remembered that I dropped mine earlier."

"Yes, of course." Hannah reached for the basket of extra silverware rolls and pulled one out. "Here you are."

But instead of taking the silverware and leaving, Edward leaned against the counter and propped himself up with an elbow. His charming smile was gone, replaced by a serious expression. In a low voice, he asked, "Did I hear you say something about the fire on the Fourth of July in 1986?"

Colt glanced at Hannah, deferring to her.

Hannah debated several replies before landing on, "Why do you ask?"

Edward looked over his shoulder at the table of Wayfinders and then dropped his voice even lower. "That's the fire that destroyed Theo's house, right?"

Hannah studied the concern in Edward's eyes. Was he worried about Theo overhearing? "Do you know much about it?"

"No more than anybody else. Terrible tragedy," Edward said, shaking his head. "I was a junior in high school when it happened. Lincoln and I were at the Fourth of July celebration with everybody else in Blackberry Valley. One moment we were having fun, and the next the town was in a state of emergency."

"Must've been awful," Hannah said.

"It was." Edward's eyes had a haunted look. "Poor Theo. I always heard the fire was caused by his mom." He turned to Colt, as though waiting for him to confirm this.

Colt shrugged and offered a polite smile. "Happened a bit before my time."

Edward returned the smile with one of his own, though it appeared strained. "Ah, sorry. I thought I heard you bring it up."

"No, I'd never heard about that particular fire. Not until Hannah was asking questions."

Edward's light blue eyes held steady on her, and she felt her cheeks grow warm under the scrutiny of his gaze. "Is this a hobby of yours?" he asked, voice light and teasing.

She forced an airy laugh. "Oh, you know. When you're marrying the fire chief, you need to know your fire history. Is there anything else I can get for you? I need to ring up the firehouse's order."

The dismissal seemed to surprise Edward—maybe it didn't happen much when one worked for the city—but he nodded a farewell to them both and returned to the table of Wayfinders.

Hannah went about filling the cups with lemonade. "Better get these filled so you can get back to the firehouse before they send out a search party."

After putting lids on all the drinks, Hannah arranged the lemonades in a cardboard carrier and transported them to the register.

"Sorry if I shouldn't have told him that you were asking about the fire," Colt said quietly once they'd reached the register and could speak a bit more privately. "I realized after I did that maybe you didn't want others to know."

Hannah pushed away the residual uneasiness she felt from the conversation with Edward and smiled reassuringly at Colt. "You've nothing to apologize for. I'm not trying to be secretive. What did you find?"

"Well, that's the confusing thing." Colt's brow furrowed. "The reason I wanted to make sure 1986 was the correct year is that I didn't see *any* records for a fire on that date. Fourth of July is a common date for fires, for obvious reasons, and we had records for a small one in '87 and three in '85, but I didn't see any for July 4, 1986."

"Huh." Hannah stared out the front windows of the Hot Spot, though she wasn't really looking at any of the passing cars or pedestrians. Maybe the fire happened so late that it was recorded on the next day? "What about July 5?"

"I thought about that too. But no, there are no records of fires at all that week."

"Well, that's peculiar. I know for a fact what date the fire occurred. So why wouldn't there be records?" Hannah grasped for possible answers to her question. "I can't think of any reason why those records would be stored elsewhere."

"Neither can I." Colt shrugged. "But this was my first time in the archive room. Who knows if I was even looking in the right spot?"

Hannah suspected Colt was being modest. After all, he'd found records for fires from 1985 and 1987. It was hard to imagine he couldn't have done the same for 1986—if they were stored where they were supposed to be.

Hannah passed the to-go bag over the counter. "Who is the best person for me to ask about how records are stored?"

Colt grinned at her. "If I were you, I'd start with your fiancé."

"And you're sure about the date?"

Liam's voice was hushed because it was after ten o'clock in Wyoming and he was sharing a room with Archer. Hannah had finished a late-night snack and changed into pajamas, but she was pacing the length of her dark apartment. As her bare feet pressed against the wide plank wood floor—original to the building—she wondered about other firemen over the years doing the same thing she was now.

"I'm positive about the date."

"I figured. Just had to ask."

On Liam's end, there was a rough, scratching sound. Hannah was pretty sure he was rubbing his hand against his chin, as he sometimes did when lost in thought.

"Sounds like you're overdue for a shave, Chief Berthold."

He chuckled. "You're correct. It was a long day, so I'm planning to do that tomorrow."

"And I'm keeping you awake," Hannah said. "I'm so sorry. Let's say good night so you can get some sleep."

"No, it's worth it to hear your voice. Let's talk for a few more minutes. Unless you're ready to hang up. I know it's after midnight there."

Hannah stifled a yawn. "It is, but I'm okay. I get to sleep in."

"Lucky," Liam said. "To answer your question, I can think of a few reasons the files might not be where Colt looked. I guess it's possible that he could be looking in the wrong place, although I agree that's unlikely considering he found the other years just fine. But it's possible that the records were filed incorrectly. Or sometimes those old files stick to one another, or slip to the bottom of the box, or accidentally get combined with another file. I've seen all of those scenarios."

Hannah's teeth pressed into her lower lip as she thought. "But there's no other box it might be in?"

"I doubt it."

Hannah reached the end of her apartment, pivoted, and paced the other direction. "Do you think there's a chance somebody took the file? Or that it never existed?"

"I'm sure it exists. There's a record of all calls we respond to, and that one would've been bigger than usual." Liam paused. "Dad would've been the fire chief then. Want me to ask him what he remembers?"

Hannah thought of the look Edward had given her, clearly thinking her strange, and her stomach tightened at the thought of Liam asking his father about this. Understandably, he'd want to know why his future daughter-in-law was curious about a particular fire from before she was even born.

"I don't know," Hannah said. "Maybe it doesn't matter."

"I don't have to say you're the one asking about it." Liam's voice was gentle. He knew her so well. "I can tell him the file isn't where it should be and ask if he knows why. No mention of you is necessary. How about that?"

"Okay, thank you," Hannah said. "I'm probably just being paranoid because Edward Lake overheard me and Colt talking about it. He was teasing me about that being a strange hobby, looking into old fires."

"Edward Lake was teasing you?"

Hannah stopped her pacing. "Why did your voice change when you asked that?"

"It's just that Edward Lake is a flirt. I suspect his supposed teasing was actually flirting," Liam said.

A laugh burst out of Hannah. "Liam Berthold, he's old enough to be my father. He definitely wasn't flirting with me."

"Even still," Liam grumbled. "Sounds like I need to get home."

Hannah started to protest and decided against it. "I've been telling you that for two weeks. You should definitely come home right away and keep an eye on Edward."

"I wish I could." Liam yawned. "I better get to bed."

"Yes, you should." Hannah dropped into her favorite armchair. "Oh, just so you know, I probably won't be able to talk tomorrow afternoon. I'm going paddleboarding with my aunt and Theo."

"Okay," Liam said around another yawn. "Wear a life vest."

Hannah smiled to herself. These kinds of responses were common when dating a first responder. "Good night, Liam."

Chapter Fifteen

Hannah awoke to the predicted thunderstorm rumbling outside her apartment. For a while she lay there and listened to the soothing sounds of distant thunder and rain splattering against her windows. She prayed Wyoming would have rain soon so the people in the area would no longer be in danger and Liam could feel confident about coming home.

While she drank her morning coffee, Hannah reviewed the things that remained on her wedding to-do list. The catering task was the biggest item that still needed crossing off. With a resigned sigh, she pulled up the caterer's contact information and made the call.

"This is Taylor Made Catering. How can I help you?"

Hannah flipped through her stack of papers, hunting for the price list. She couldn't believe someone had *actually* answered the phone. "Hi, this is Hannah Prentiss. I'm returning Taylor's phone call."

"Hi, Hannah!" The voice on the other end of the phone turned warm. "I'm so embarrassed by how long we've been trying to connect with each other. Thanks for being patient with me. If you give me just a second, I'll pull up my notes from our first call."

By lunchtime, Hannah had negotiated a good price and booked the caterer, reserved linens for the reception, and compiled several centerpiece ideas that she thought would be ideal for a fall wedding and easy to do herself.

When she texted Liam excitedly about everything she'd accomplished that morning, he sent her a screenshot of his weather app. Rain was expected in Wyoming, and it was supposed to last for much of the day.

What a fantastic start to her Thursday.

By the time Hannah left to meet Aunt Fiona and the others at Lake Blackberry, the skies were light blue and the air far less humid than usual. Raindrops clung to the leaves and flowers, making them sparkle in the sun.

When she crested the hill and saw Lake Blackberry glittering below, Hannah spotted several small boats and paddleboards already out on the water. She pulled into the paddleboard rental shop and found only her aunt and Theo outside with vests and three boards.

Hannah grabbed her keys and phone but left her purse tucked under the passenger seat before she climbed out.

Aunt Fiona waved to her. "I hope it's okay that we went ahead and got the boards."

"Of course," Hannah said. "Where are the others? I thought there was a whole group coming."

"That's what we were hoping, but it didn't work out that way. Your brother had to work, Allison had already agreed to watch a friend's baby this afternoon, your dad was taking Zeus for his yearly appointment, and..." Aunt Fiona frowned up at Theo. "I don't remember what Gordon said. Do you?"

Theo shrugged and adjusted his hat. "I think he just wasn't interested."

Hannah felt a bit like a third wheel on a date, but there wasn't much she could do about that now. "Well, thanks for inviting me along. It's been ages since I last paddleboarded."

Theo lifted the long board with an air of expertise. "I'm happy you could join us. So you've done this before?"

Hannah slipped her arms through the holes of her life vest. "Only twice."

"Theo paddleboards frequently." Aunt Fiona beamed up at him. "But I've never been on one."

Even so, Aunt Fiona hoisted her board with impressive ease and followed Theo down to the shore. Hannah was glad neither of them were watching as she picked up her own board, struggled to gain control of it and then trotted along behind.

They took their time getting into the water. Theo suggested Aunt Fiona should start on her knees rather than standing, just until she got a feel for being on the water. Aunt Fiona followed this advice, but barely two minutes later, she stood, looking solid as a statue.

"You'll be doing yoga poses on that board within the hour," Hannah said as she forced herself to stand as well. She remained upright, but her knees wobbled.

Theo nodded approvingly at Aunt Fiona. "Your daily yoga practice is probably very helpful in this situation. Good core strength and balance."

Aunt Fiona gave a modest shrug. "Being short also means I have a lower center of gravity. That has to help as well."

Hannah was pretty sure her aunt was just trying to make her feel better.

"Do you both feel comfortable enough to paddle across the lake?" Theo asked, gliding alongside them with enviable ease. "I'd like to see where my house was. I had a rope tied to a big tree over there, and I used to swing into the lake. I assume it's long gone—or the rope is anyway—but I'd like to paddle over all the same."

"Sounds good to me," Aunt Fiona said.

"Sure," Hannah agreed.

Theo led their group at a slower pace than what Hannah suspected he was capable of—not that she was complaining. By the time they arrived on the other side of the lake, she felt more comfortable on the board and her knees no longer trembled, but many of the muscles in her arms and back protested all the extra work.

As they approached the house Aunt Fiona had pointed out to Hannah, Theo lifted his oar out of the water and drifted.

"Remarkable," he said to the two of them. "There's absolutely nothing familiar. I thought there might be when I was looking at it from the water, but no. Even the tree is gone."

Hannah shielded her eyes and squinted in the bright sunlight. A woman paced along the expansive back deck of the huge house. She wore a tailored dress, had short, dark hair, and held a cell phone against her ear as she walked. There was something familiar about her, but she was too far away for Hannah to see her clearly.

"The town has grown and changed a lot," Aunt Fiona said as she ceased paddling. "Even places that haven't been completely renovated seem different to me."

"Yeah, I suppose you're right." But Theo continued to look up at the house with his jaw clenched. "I wonder if my mom will even recognize it this weekend."

"Your mom is coming this weekend?" Hannah asked. She shot a look at Aunt Fiona, but her aunt must've already known because she didn't seem surprised.

"She is." Theo smiled and glanced at Aunt Fiona. "She's wanted to come back for a while now, and when she found out Fiona was here, that sealed the deal."

"I think you're exaggerating," Fiona said. "Mind if we sit and drift for a bit? My arms could use a rest."

"Mine too," Hannah agreed. Since she was younger than them by nearly two decades, she hadn't wanted to be the first to ask for a break, but she definitely needed one. "If you don't have plans already, you should bring your mom to the Hot Spot for dinner. I'd love to meet her."

"I'm sure she'd enjoy that." Theo gave her a kind smile. "She always got on well with your grandparents."

After a bit of silence, Hannah said, "Theo, I hope I'm not prying when I ask this, but can you think of any reason why the Blackberry Valley Fire Department would have no records of the fire at your house?"

Theo turned to her. "They have *no* record?" She couldn't see his eyes behind his sunglasses, but by the tone of his voice, she could tell he was surprised.

"I guess it's premature to say they have no records," Hannah corrected herself. "But they couldn't find the file. I spoke to Chief Berthold about it, and he said it's possible that it was misplaced. I was curious if you had other ideas."

Aunt Fiona's eyes twinkled. "Do you always call your fiancé 'Chief Berthold?'"

Hannah smiled at her aunt. "No, but I thought it might be confusing for Theo if I just called him Liam."

Theo stared off into the distance and then shook his head. "I can't think of why they might not have a record of it. That's strange."

Conversation ceased, and there were only the sounds of the water lapping against the shore and the occasional voice of the woman on the deck.

"The fire *did* happen a long time ago," Aunt Fiona said. "Over the course of forty years, a lot of things can happen to a file."

"True," Theo murmured, staring into the water. Then he maneuvered his board to face Hannah. "Why did you ask the fire department about it?"

He didn't sound angry, but even still Hannah said, "I'm sorry if I overstepped. I did it because I wondered if any new information came out after you and your mom moved away. Information that might help release you from any lingering guilt that you might feel."

Theo pushed his sunglasses on top of his head. "That was kind of you. I've always assumed that if anything else of importance was discovered, Kenneth would've reached out. But it was thoughtful of you to check all the same."

"Do you think your mom would have any records of the fire?" Aunt Fiona asked, her face pensive.

Theo huffed a sound that was something like a laugh. "Mom isn't really the type to keep records. And even if she did, I don't know what helpful information would be in there. I tried speaking to her a few days ago about the fire."

"Did it upset her?" Aunt Fiona asked.

"I couldn't tell. She didn't change the subject, like she usually does."

Hannah's eyes tracked the dark-haired woman on the deck as she reentered her home, then her gaze drifted to where Aunt Fiona's paddleboard bumped up against Theo's.

"They're going to continue looking for the file," Hannah said. "And Liam told me he'd ask his father—the previous Chief Berthold—if he has ideas of other places the records might be."

Theo's smile was slight but sincere. "I wish I thought there'd be something in there that would put Mom's mind at ease. All these years later, she still feels guilty." He shook his head. "It makes me sad. She was a wonderful mother. Flawed, yes, but wonderful."

"Of course she was." Aunt Fiona reached beyond her board and clasped Theo's hand. "We all have flaws. And even if she *is* responsible for the fire, it was a mistake. Mistakes happen."

Theo smiled at Aunt Fiona with such tenderness that Hannah felt compelled to look away and offer them what little privacy she could. As she directed her gaze back toward the house, she saw a boxy, bright yellow vehicle pull away.

Hannah remembered seeing the canary-colored Jeep in the garage of the same house over the weekend, when she'd come by with Aunt Fiona. The SUV had seemed familiar because she'd seen it a few days prior at the Hot Spot. It was the Jeep that belonged to Courtney Underhill.

Hannah gazed up at the big house. "Theo, are you sure this is the property the rental house was on?"

Theo looked up at the house. "Pretty sure, yeah. Why?"

"Any idea who lives here now?"

"No. Why?"

Hannah hesitated. If she was wrong, she hated to stir up trouble. “I’m not one hundred percent sure, but I think that was Courtney Underhill walking around on the deck a few minutes ago. She’s in charge of Lawrence Underhill Properties now and is the daughter of Lawrence Underhill.”

Theo’s brow furrowed.

Hannah was surprised to see that Aunt Fiona didn’t appear to be paying attention to them. Instead, she had her cell phone out of her dry bag.

“It’s a little odd, don’t you think?” Hannah said. “That they would live here now?”

“Maybe. I suppose it’s worth looking into,” Theo said slowly. “Though I’m not really sure how to figure out if—”

“Jennifer, hello! How are you?”

Hannah nearly toppled off her paddleboard at the sound of Aunt Fiona’s loud, cheerful voice. Her aunt had her cell phone pressed to her ear. What a bizarre time to make a phone call.

“Yes, isn’t this weather glorious?” Aunt Fiona continued, seeming oblivious to Hannah’s and Theo’s stares. “Feels more like July in Colorado than it does Kentucky. Makes a girl want to move home. Speaking of which, I was in your neighborhood recently, and there’s a gorgeous brick house right on the lake with a huge deck out back. Do you know who that belongs to?”

Hannah stifled a laugh and then glanced at Theo and found him watching Aunt Fiona with a bemused expression.

Aunt Fiona’s laugh rang loud. “Oh, I wish. Not with my nurse’s salary, I’m afraid. But it doesn’t stop me from admiring impressive architecture when I see it. The house I'm talking about is one of the first ones you come to if you're turning onto Blackbird Road."

Aunt Fiona listened for a moment, and Hannah could tell by the way her expression darkened that Hannah's guess had been right. For several minutes, Aunt Fiona said nothing more than "hmm" and "oh, really?" to whatever Jennifer said.

Finally, Aunt Fiona said, "That's interesting. Sorry to have taken you away from your class. I'll let you return to that, but let's get coffee before I leave town, okay?"

When Aunt Fiona pulled the phone away from her ear, she smiled affectionately at it. "That was a high school friend of mine. She was Jennifer Martin back then, but she's Jennifer Hornberger now. Do you remember her, Theo?"

Theo shook his head.

"She was at my birthday party. The one with the very red hair? She had those big bangs in high school."

Theo shook his head again, and Hannah did as well. The names and faces of Aunt Fiona's high school friends had all started to blur together at some point in the evening.

"Anyway." Aunt Fiona secured her phone in the dry bag and closed it. "Sweet Jennifer never could resist a ringing telephone. She picked up in the middle of a Pilates class. She said that house is owned by Lawrence Underhill and his wife, though it's his daughter living there now."

Hannah grimaced.

"I guess it isn't too surprising," Theo said, the words emerging slowly, as if he was thinking about each one as he spoke it. "They owned the property after all, and it was an empty lot after the fire. Why not build a big, beautiful house on it?"

"Maybe," Aunt Fiona said. "But I still think it's strange."

Theo considered this. "I think you're being defensive of me and my mom. The longer I think about it, the more sense it makes. He was in the business of real estate development. This wasn't going to be a good spot to build apartments or a retail center or anything of that nature."

Hannah could follow the train of thought. "That's true. And it would've been zoned for a residence. I don't know much about real estate, but I'm guessing building a new house and renting it out doesn't make much financial sense."

"I wouldn't think so," Theo said.

Hannah gazed at the back of the enormous house. "So, the choices would've been to sell the lot or to build a house he wanted to live in."

He nodded, but Aunt Fiona still wore a grim expression. "I don't like it."

Theo smiled affectionately at her. "The man could've made life really hard for my mom, and he didn't. I'm not going to begrudge his right to build himself a mansion."

"Sure, but just because you're being the bigger person doesn't mean I have to be," Aunt Fiona said with a teasing smile.

Hannah's cell phone rang from the dry bag strapped to the end of her board. She thought the call might end up in voicemail with how long it took her to retrieve her phone, but thankfully she was able to answer Elaine's call in time.

"Hi, Elaine. How are you?"

"Hannah." Elaine's voice was tight, as though she was holding back tears. "How fast can you be at the restaurant?"

Hannah looked into the distance, where she knew her Subaru was parked. Just seeing the dots of cars on the distant shore made her arms ache. "It'll take me a bit. I'm out on Lake Blackberry. What's going on?"

"The city inspector is here," Elaine said. "The Hot Spot is being shut down."

Chapter Sixteen

If it were an ordinary afternoon, Hannah would have felt embarrassed to run along the sidewalk of Main Street wearing flip-flops, her paddleboarding clothes, and the messiest of messy buns. But this wasn't an ordinary afternoon, and she didn't give her appearance much more than a second thought as she sprinted down the sidewalk and yanked the door open.

Elaine, Jacob, Raquel, and Dylan sat huddled in a corner booth, and all four looked up with big eyes when she rushed inside.

"He's already left," Elaine said as Hannah drew closer. "I tried to keep him here until you arrived, but he had other appointments."

Hannah couldn't blame the city inspector for not sticking around. Paddling across Lake Blackberry had taken twenty minutes, followed by another ten minutes of dragging their boards out of the water and up to the clubhouse. Theo and Aunt Fiona insisted on returning her board for her, and Hannah had been too worried about the Hot Spot to protest. Even so, the drive to town was a solid twenty minutes, and all of that added up to a very long time to ask a city inspector to wait.

Hannah looked at her staff—the people whose livelihoods depended on her—and squelched her desire to know everything that had transpired while she was away. All she'd taken the time to learn from Elaine was that this wasn't a health department issue, but rather something to do with a change of city code. After that, she'd hung up so she could start paddling. Even now, the extra details would have to wait because they only had an hour until customers would begin arriving.

"The first thing we need to do is put something on social media. Dylan?" Hannah unlocked her phone and passed it to the young man. "Write up something along the lines of, 'Due to unforeseen circumstances, the Hot Spot will be closed today. Sorry for the inconvenience.' As soon as you've posted, we can all get on our personal accounts and share."

Dylan wordlessly took her phone and began tapping.

"Raquel, please go to my office, get on my laptop, and print a sign that says something similar and post it on the door. 'Closed today. Sorry for the inconvenience.'"

Raquel slid off her seat. "Sure thing."

Hannah turned to her hostess next. "Elaine, do you remember how to change the recording on our phone line?"

Elaine nodded, her earrings swinging with the motion.

"Okay, great. Update it with similar messaging so we don't have frustrated callers hoping to place a to-go order."

"You got it."

With the others gone and Dylan's attention on Hannah's phone, Hannah faced Jacob. His stricken expression and tight jaw made her own emotions swell dangerously close to the surface. "Tell me what happened," she said softly.

Jacob swallowed hard. "I'd only been here a few minutes when a city inspector arrived. Someone I didn't recognize. He told Elaine he needed to look at our grease trap."

Hannah frowned. "But we don't have a grease trap."

"That's what I told him, and that's when he said he'd have to shut us down until we had one installed and inspected. He said all restaurants are required to have grease traps."

Hannah inhaled deeply for the first time since she'd gotten off her call with Elaine. This wasn't as big a deal as she'd initially thought. "This must be a misunderstanding."

Jacob gave her a skeptical look. "He seemed pretty sure of himself."

"I'll call and get this sorted out. The Hot Spot isn't required to have a grease trap because of the historic status of our building. I had this conversation with the city before we opened. Getting a grease trap installed here would involve excavation work, which would risk the integrity of the building. Fortunately, the city also wanted to preserve the building, and they said the Hot Spot could be excused from the normal regulations."

Jacob's frown persisted. "I don't know, Hannah. He said this was a serious violation and seemed really confident that we'd be shut down until we could get a grease trap installed."

"That may be, but *I'm* confident this is a misunderstanding. I assume he left a phone number or some way for me to contact him?"

"Elaine has his card." Jacob rubbed at the perpetual scruff on his jaw. "He *was* on the young side. I wouldn't be surprised if he graduated from college in May and this is his first job."

Hannah reached into her back pocket for her phone to check the time, only to remember that Dylan currently had her device and was working his magic on social media. "I'll get this sorted out, and we'll hopefully still be able to open tonight. For sure by tomorrow."

Jacob still appeared doubtful. "I hope so. I hate to think of having to turn away customers."

So did Hannah. Visions of an empty dining room had plagued her thoughts for the entire drive from Lake Blackberry. "Don't worry, Jacob. Why don't you go to the kitchen and see if there's anything simple for the staff to eat?"

The idea of returning to the kitchen smoothed out the creases in his forehead, and she knew that the familiar rhythms of cooking would soothe him further. Not that she felt like she could eat a single bite.

Hannah retrieved her phone from Dylan, left him stationed at the door with instructions to stay there until Raquel finished the sign, and then she went to where Elaine stood at the counter they used for to-go orders. Elaine was hanging up the phone as Hannah approached.

"The new recording is running," Elaine said. "People can still leave messages, but it says we're not currently taking orders."

"Okay, thanks. I'll monitor it carefully, because it's not unheard of for someone to leave a to-go order in a voicemail and expect it to be ready fifteen minutes later. But I'm optimistic that we won't be shut down for long."

Elaine cocked her head and studied Hannah. "Yes, I can tell. Why's that?"

"Jacob said this is about the grease trap. We don't need a grease trap because of our historic building."

"What's a grease trap?" Elaine asked.

"It's a tank that does exactly what you might think—it traps grease in the restaurant's wastewater before it enters the system. They're a good idea, and most cities require them, but installing them in a historic property can cause structural issues. I cleared us not installing one with the city long before we opened. I think this inspector just didn't know about the exception. Do you have his contact info for me?"

"Right here." Elaine reached into her pocket and withdrew a business card. The card was thin and cheap, with the Blackberry Valley city logo in the top left and the name of the employee printed in bold caps across the middle.

"Braylon Hooper," Hannah read as she used her thumb to enter the phone number on her keypad. "I don't think I know any Hoopers. You?"

Elaine shook her head. A line had appeared between her brows, as it did when she was thinking hard or worried. "I'd never seen him before. He was really young too. If I'd seen him around town, I would've thought he was still in college."

"College grads all look so young to me these days." Hannah pressed the phone to her ear as it rang. "It's hard to believe I was that young when I moved across the country on my own, because I felt so—"

"This is Braylon," answered a male voice.

Hannah infused her own voice with warmth. "Hello, Braylon. This is Hannah Prentiss, owner of the Hot Spot. Is now a good time to talk?"

There was a moment's hesitation on the other end of the line. Maybe her voice sounded a little *too* warm, as if she weren't taking this seriously.

"Yes. I assume you're calling to discuss the mandate."

"I am."

"As I explained to your staff, the city of Blackberry Valley requires all restaurants to have grease traps. This helps our water treatment facilities to serve us all better. You will be able to reopen as soon as the grease trap is installed and has been inspected by the city. Do you understand?"

"Actually, Braylon, I think there's been a misunderstanding. Due to the historic status of our building, the city decided we're not required to have a grease trap. That decision was made before I opened, so if you need to look up records, then check in the spring of—"

"That may be, but regulations have changed, ma'am. Your restaurant will need to remain closed until a grease trap has been installed and inspected by the city."

Hannah inhaled deeply and put on the voice she typically reserved for customers who were being difficult. "I don't know how long you've held your job, but this agreement was made before I opened the restaurant—"

"Ma'am, I understand you're under the impression that this rule doesn't apply to you and your restaurant, but I assure you it does."

His terse words made Hannah feel as though she'd been slapped across the face. She wasn't going to get anywhere talking to this guy. He was so confident that he wouldn't even listen to her. "Is there someone else I can speak to?"

Braylon sighed. "I can give you my supervisor's number, but he's just going to tell you the same thing. The fastest way to get your restaurant open again is to get a grease trap installed."

Hannah reached for the order pad she kept by the restaurant's phone and tried to ignore the concerned look Elaine gave her. "All the same, I'd like your supervisor's name and number."

The inspector rattled off the number, and then said, "His name is Edward Lake."

"Great," Hannah said, and she meant it. Not only had Edward been part of the initial decision that the Hot Spot didn't need a grease trap, but he ate at the Hot Spot regularly. There was no way he'd want the Hot Spot closed. "I'll give him a call now."

Hannah ended her call with Braylon before he could reply.

Elaine stood with her arms crossed, as if to hold herself together. The line between her eyebrows had deepened. "That didn't sound like it went well."

Hannah smiled at Elaine, hoping it came across as reassuring but without overconfidence. "Everything will be fine. Braylon is convinced he's right, but his supervisor is Edward Lake. Edward is the one who approved the exception when we were opening, so this should take care of the problem. I'm calling him now, and he'll get things sorted out."

As she waited for Edward to answer, Hannah watched Raquel breeze through the room holding a piece of paper in one hand and a roll of tape in the other. Should she tell Raquel not to bother? This grease trap nonsense would be over as soon as she explained the situation to Edward and reminded him of the decision the city had made back when she was going through the process of applying for permits and getting plans approved.

"Hi, you've reached the office of Edward Lake. I'm not available to take your call right now..."

Hannah frowned as his recorded voice continued. As soon as the beep sounded, she put on a smile and a confident tone. "Hello, Edward. This is Hannah Prentiss at the Hot Spot. One of the city inspectors was here today—Braylon—and he appears to be confused about some of the regulations. If you can call me back as soon as you're able, that would be great. Thank you."

She tacked on both the Hot Spot's phone number as well as that of her cell phone and then hung up.

Elaine bit her fingernail. "Maybe he's already left work for the day?"

"I'm sure he's still there. It's not even four yet." Hannah's teeth pressed into her lower lip. "It'll be fine. He'll return my call before he goes home for the day."

Wouldn't he? She should've made it clearer that he needed to call her immediately, not just "as soon as possible." If he didn't call her back, then they had no chance of opening tonight. And there would be uncertainty heading into tomorrow. Being closed on a Friday would be a terrible hit to their finances. She imagined the glowing red numbers in the accounting software.

"Actually, it's not that far of a walk to the city offices. I'll go there now."

This statement only seemed to make Elaine more nervous. Hannah tried for another everything-is-fine kind of smile, but it felt weak.

Hannah spent her five-minute walk rehearsing what she would say to Edward. As she approached the brick building, she caught sight of her reflection in the glass door. Her jean shorts and flip flops didn't give her the appearance of a woman who should be taken seriously.

That didn't matter, she reminded herself. She was on the right side of the law here, and she didn't need to be dressed a certain way to remind the city of what they'd already agreed to.

She pulled open the front door and cast a warm smile at the receptionist. "Hello. I'm here to see Edward Lake."

The receptionist was young, with a long ponytail and stylishly oversize glasses. She appeared to be comparing two documents, and she pressed a bright pink fingernail onto each page to mark her spot before looking up at Hannah. "He's gone for the day. Would you like to leave a message?"

Gone for the day? Hannah internally groaned. "This is an urgent matter. Do you have his cell number?"

The young woman blinked at her. "We don't give out personal information, ma'am."

"Right, of course not." So now there was *no* chance of opening the Hot Spot tonight. Hannah fought back her panic. This situation wasn't the receptionist's fault, and it would do no good to make an enemy of her. Hannah fixed her smile into place. "What time do you expect him tomorrow?"

"Let me check." The receptionist swiveled toward her computer where she did a lot of mouse clicking. Hannah could see the reflections of various calendars in her large glasses. "Looks like Mr. Lake is out of the office tomorrow."

"Out?" Hannah's heart sank. "All day?"

"Yes," the receptionist confirmed.

This time Hannah did groan. "Any chance he works on Saturdays?"

"No, ma'am."

"No, I didn't think so," Hannah muttered.

This was really bad. If she couldn't speak to Edward and get this misunderstanding cleared up by tomorrow, that would mean the Hot Spot would be closed not just Friday night but Saturday night as well.

"It's critical that I speak with him," Hannah said. "There's been a terrible misunderstanding, and my restaurant has been wrongfully shut down. I won't be able to reopen until I speak with Edward."

"You could speak to someone on his staff instead." The receptionist clicked her mouse a few times. "Let's see. It seems Braylon Hooper is the staff member in charge of food service regulations."

"I've already spoken to Braylon. I *have* to speak to Edward."

"Sorry, ma'am. I can schedule an appointment for you on Monday, if you'd like."

Monday.

The thought of how much food they'd have to throw away nauseated Hannah. Nearly all their fresh ingredients would have to be pitched—they couldn't count on being able to use them come Tuesday night. Additionally, they would lose an entire weekend of profits, which couldn't be recouped, and her staff would lose three nights—tonight through Saturday—of work hours and tips.

The weight of the situation felt heavy upon her shoulders.

"Is there really no one else I can talk to?"

The receptionist shook her head. "I'm sorry, there's not. We're a skeleton crew in the summer, like a lot of places."

Hannah sighed deeply. A headache had blossomed at the base of her skull. What else could she do? Nothing.

"What's the earliest appointment Edward has available on Monday?"

Hannah trudged back to the Hot Spot with nothing more to show for her time than a meeting scheduled for eight a.m., four long days from now.

Chapter Seventeen

Hannah poked at a slice of key lime pie that she wasn't in the mood to eat and watched Zeus scamper along the fence, hunting for squirrels. Also sitting around the table on the back deck were her dad and Uncle Gordon, who were debating the benefits of citronella candles versus having a company spray the yard for mosquitos. Hannah was lost in her own thoughts and only kind of listening. Aunt Fiona had been sitting with them, but she'd walked away a few minutes ago to take a phone call.

After walking back to the Hot Spot from the city offices, Hannah had told her staff in as confident a voice as she could manage that, no, she hadn't made progress yet, but she was sure that as soon as she spoke with Edward, everything would be sorted out.

"So, enjoy your unexpected night off," Hannah said with a forced smile.

Her staff weakly smiled back at her and said reassuring things before they left.

Up in her apartment, she called Liam first. When he didn't answer, she tried Lacy. They'd talked for nearly an hour and then Neil had arrived home. Hannah told her friend to enjoy her evening and tried calling Liam again. He'd answered that time, but he was in a truck with six other firemen, so it wasn't a great conversation. She told him everything that had happened, and then he had to go.

Feeling lonely, Hannah had made a snap decision to drive to her dad's house. She grabbed a key lime pie from the Hot Spot refrigerator and arrived just in time for dinner. Dad, Uncle Gordon, and Aunt Fiona were all outraged on her behalf, and Hannah was grateful for the company.

But she really missed Liam.

Aunt Fiona reappeared on the deck, her bare feet slapping against the wood. She wore a bright smile as she held her cell phone out to Hannah. "It's Edward Lake. Rusty gave me his number. He's in the middle of a golf game right now, but I told him this is an emergency."

Hannah stared at the outstretched phone and could have wept with gratitude. "Oh, bless you." She pulled Aunt Fiona's phone to her ear and said brightly, "Edward?"

There was a moment's hesitation and then Edward said, "Yes?"

"This is Hannah Prentiss, owner of the Hot Spot. How are you this evening?" Hannah pushed herself out of the chair and headed inside the house for privacy.

"I'm fine, thanks for asking." Another hesitation. "Fiona said this is an emergency?"

"Yes. There's been a misunderstanding at the Hot Spot, and I need your help clearing it up."

With that, the story spooled out of her in a long, continuous ribbon. She told him what Braylon had said and how this directly contradicted what the city had decided when the Hot Spot opened, then reminded Edward of the historic status of the building.

When she'd reached the end, Edward said nothing. Probably because she'd spoken for so long that he might not realize she'd said everything she needed to.

"I'm hoping you can bring some much-needed clarity to the situation," she added.

"Thank you for explaining all that to me." Edward's tone was soft and understanding. "I can see how this whole situation would feel very confusing and stressful."

Hannah already felt calmer. She sank onto her dad's favorite chair and released a long sigh. "Thank you, Edward. I tried explaining to Braylon multiple times that an exception had been made for the Hot Spot, but he was insistent. Which I understand," she rushed on. "He was doing his job. He just didn't know better."

"Well, Hannah." Edward cleared his throat. "I hate to be the bearer of bad news, but Braylon was correct. At a council meeting four months ago, a decision was made that all restaurants must have grease traps, regardless of their circumstances."

Dread sank low in Hannah's gut. She needed to say something, but "Oh," was all she could manage.

"I'm awfully sorry about how you're finding out. It certainly sounds like our office could've done a better job communicating that you're now in violation of the code. I'll make a note to discuss that with the office on Monday."

Hannah stared at the coffee table, not really seeing it. Tears clogged her throat, and she swallowed hard. "Are you saying that we actually do have to shut down and get a grease trap installed?"

"I know it's an inconvenience, Hannah—"

"It's a lot more than an inconvenience." Hannah's panic had taken over her brain and was now running the show. "Do you realize this means we'll have to be shut down at least a week, and that's only if I can find a company that can come out in the next day or two and give us an estimate? I have staff I won't be able to pay, a kitchen full of food that will have to be thrown away, and on top of all that, I'll somehow have to dig up thousands of dollars to pay for the grease trap to be installed. Why wasn't the change communicated to me before?" Not that it would have helped.

"I'll tell you what, Hannah. Let me have a few conversations and see what I can do for you. I'm not promising that I can make this problem go away entirely, but I'll do what I can. In the meantime, I advise that you still make some calls to area plumbers. Sometimes these situations are easier to manage if we can show that you're playing ball, you know?"

She should be grateful. Edward didn't owe her anything. He could've just said *No, this is the way things are*, and then Hannah would've had zero hope about the next couple of weeks. This was better than nothing.

Even so, she was having a hard time not feeling angry with him. Especially when she knew that after they hung up, he'd be returning to his golf game while she tried to figure out whether there was any way to pay her staff.

"Thank you," she said, somewhat stiffly.

"It's my pleasure. I'll call you as soon as I know something more."

"Okay, thank you. This is actually my aunt's phone, so let me give you a better..."

Hannah trailed off and held the phone where she could see the screen. As she suspected, the words *Call ended* blinked below the phone number. That was okay. If he called back—*when* he called back, rather—he would reach Aunt Fiona, who would pass along her contact info.

Even so, Hannah texted the contact card to herself. Now at least she could call him. Hannah knew that the phrase "the squeaky wheel gets the grease" was absolutely true, and she felt no reservations about squeaking more if it helped to get the Hot Spot reopened.

After taking a moment to pray for swift results, Hannah walked back outside to the deck, where Dad, Uncle Gordon, and Aunt Fiona sat around the table. Aunt Fiona was in the middle of sharing about Theo's mom coming into town, but she stopped speaking as soon as Hannah stepped outside. They all looked at her, faces bright with hopeful expectation. Hannah turned away, knowing she was about to disappoint them.

"Thank you, Aunt Fiona," she said as she returned her aunt's phone.

"Of course. What'd he say, honey?"

Hannah took her seat and forced herself to hold her head high rather than slouch in defeat. "Edward said there was a change to the regulations a few months ago, so we actually do have to comply with a new grease trap law."

"What?" Aunt Fiona cried.

"That's ridiculous," her dad scoffed.

Both responses were amusing, since neither of them had known what a grease trap was an hour ago.

Uncle Gordon, a retired plumber, just gave a solemn nod. "I know some guys who will give you the best price they can and take care with the historic building, Hannah. I'll put you in touch."

"Thanks, Uncle Gordon." Hannah did her best to smile at him.

He leaned back in his seat, a thoughtful expression on his face. "Still, I'm surprised the city isn't willing to work with you on this.

Seems to me like they would've notified you about the change and given you time to comply *before* they walked in and shut you down."

Dad and Aunt Fiona chimed in with their agreement.

"When I explained in detail what this meant for the Hot Spot, Edward said that he would talk to some people at the city and see what he could do—"

Dad snorted. "Sounds like politician speak for 'do nothing' to me."

"—but even so, it'd be good for me to get estimates." Hannah stopped trying to look as though she didn't feel defeated. It was okay to be real with these three. "The worst part is having to be closed for so long. What am I going to do about my staff? They depend on me. They have bills to pay, same as I do. They can't afford to miss a week's salary—maybe more—and I can't afford to pay them with the restaurant closed."

Aunt Fiona's hand closed over hers. "You're so smart, Hannah. I know we can figure this out. Rusty will help you crunch the numbers."

That may be, but Rusty couldn't make dollars appear out of thin air.

Chapter Eighteen

Hannah's eyes were so dry that they ached, no doubt because she'd only managed a few hours of sleep last night.

This morning when she'd awoken, she'd felt better about the situation. In fact, she thought maybe this could even be a blessing. Didn't she have a tremendous number of items on her to-do list? Didn't she sometimes think "if I could take a week off from running the restaurant, then I'd have time to…" And here she was with an indeterminate amount of time off. When viewed in that light, this was an opportunity.

However, hours later, her enthusiasm had waned. She'd left messages for several local plumbing companies Uncle Gordon had recommended. Now she had to wait for them to call her back. She'd come into her office with the intention of making updates to the Hot Spot website, but instead she'd been on the phone with Liam for half an hour. The initial part of the call had involved a lot of ranting, but then he made a sharp turn into problem-solving mode.

"Edward isn't the only person who knows people at the city. I do too," he said in the no-nonsense voice he adopted in crisis situations. "I'll make some phone calls and see what I can do."

"Really? I know you're busy up there."

"Not too busy for you. And even if ultimately, you *do* need to install the grease trap, I don't see why you need to be closed between now and then. This isn't a health code violation, and no one told you about the change in policy. It's not unreasonable to ask for a window of time to comply. Maybe they would agree to you staying open, so long as you have an installation scheduled for some time in the next thirty days."

Hannah nodded along. "That's what Dad and Uncle Gordon think too, but I wasn't thinking like that when I was on the phone with Edward last night."

There were muffled voices on the other end. "I'm so sorry, but I have to go," Liam said. "Don't worry, honey. We'll figure this out."

More than anything, she wanted Liam to come home. But how could she ask that of him when he was doing so much good for others in Wyoming? She couldn't.

"I know," she said instead. "Stay safe."

Hannah put her phone away and tried to ignore the melancholic pull of her thoughts. She redirected her attention to the website, clicking each link to ensure it worked properly, but her thoughts kept wandering. The Hot Spot was always closed at eleven a.m. on Fridays, but still there was something about being in her office and knowing the restaurant wasn't going to open that night that made focusing on her task extra challenging. It was as if her brain knew the usual deadline of when she needed to get work done didn't exist that day.

Her phone buzzed, and she smiled at the sight of Lacy's all caps, angry texts responding to the update Hannah had sent her about her conversation with Edward. While Lacy's outrage could do nothing to expedite the opening of the restaurant, it was still meaningful that she cared so much.

Hannah texted back and then checked the restaurant's social media, where she responded to the numerous comments left on the Hot Spot post Dylan had created yesterday afternoon. Nearly all the responses were supportive, though someone had piped in with an unhelpful story about a time when the health department had shut down a local restaurant due to a cockroach infestation. Hannah rushed to reply that this had nothing to do with the health department, and there were definitely no infestations at the Hot Spot.

By the time she looked at her computer again, it had gone to sleep.

Hannah sighed. "Time for a change of scenery," she murmured into the quiet of her office.

She tucked her phone in her back pocket, packed up her laptop, and walked to Jump Start Coffee. The summer air was thick, but there was a nice breeze, and the sky was full of puffy white clouds, like a child's painting.

Zane Forrest, Jacob's brother, stood behind the register. The brothers looked similar, although Zane wore glasses and had a short, well-maintained beard. Both usually had the same full smile, but when Hannah entered, Zane gave her a tempered variety, as if they were seeing each other at a funeral.

"How are you today?" he asked.

Hannah tried to make her own smile appear normal. "I'm okay. How are you?"

"Better than you, I'm guessing." Zane leaned against the counter. "Jacob was over at my house last night, venting about what happened."

"It was a rough afternoon." Hannah heard the door jingle as it opened behind her, announcing the arrival of someone else. "Can I get an iced coffee with cream, please? Large."

Zane pulled a cup from the stack and wrote on the side with a marker. "You got it."

Hannah reached into her purse for her wallet, but Zane waved her away.

"Not today."

"Zane, no—"

But he shook his head and handed the cup to the barista. "It's the least I can do."

Zane's kind gesture made Hannah want to cry, which was more evidence of her short night of sleep.

Hannah put her wallet away. "Thanks, Zane."

She stepped away from the register with a glance over her shoulder at whoever had come in behind her. It was Courtney Underhill, dressed as always in a skirt suit and heels. Hannah smiled at her, but Courtney appeared to be lost in her own thoughts and didn't notice.

That was fine. Hannah was here to work, not socialize.

She selected a table in the middle of the coffee shop and set up her laptop. Hopefully if she was visible to everyone, that would help hold her accountable and she'd stay focused. And she faced the door so that if Edward happened to swing into Jump Start today, she could seize the opportunity.

Hannah had barely connected to the Wi-Fi when the barista called out, "Large iced coffee!"

She stood and approached the counter at the same time as Courtney, whose shoes made an authoritative clicking sound as she walked. Hannah slowed as Courtney reached to take what Hannah assumed was her own iced coffee, but the barista shook her head.

"Courtney, I'm making the soy milk iced coffee now for you. This one is Hannah's."

Courtney gave an embarrassed laugh and smiled apologetically at Hannah. "Sorry about that. I was overeager, apparently."

Hannah returned the smile as she took her coffee from the counter. "I understand. I often feel that way about coffee."

Courtney's head tilted slightly as she studied Hannah. "You look very familiar to me."

"I own the Hot Spot restaurant. My name is Hannah Prentiss."

"Yes." Courtney's face lit with recognition. "We met a few days ago."

Hannah swallowed a sip of her coffee. "That's right."

"And do you also attend Grace Community Church? I was there for the first time on Sunday, and I think I saw you."

Hannah couldn't help but brighten at the thought that she was making a new friend. "Yes, I do."

"I've only been the one time, but it seemed like a wonderful church. And I love your restaurant. It's exactly what this town needed."

Any other time, Courtney's kind words would've made Hannah glow with happiness. Instead, she was tempted to explain why the restaurant was going to be closed for a while and that it wasn't her fault, but she swallowed the urge. She didn't mind complaining about the situation to her family or Liam or Lacy, but she didn't want to come across to Courtney as a negative, whining person.

Instead, she just said, "Thank you."

"Do you own your building, or do you rent?" Courtney asked, followed immediately by a laugh. "Sorry, professional curiosity."

Hannah chuckled. "I own it. Though if I were going to rent from someone, I'd want it to be from you. I hear you're a wonderful landlady. You met my server, who lives in an apartment of yours. She was extremely grateful for the new washer and dryer in her unit. I've never seen someone look so thrilled about doing their laundry."

Courtney's cheeks turned a pleasant pink color. A new iced coffee was placed on the counter, and Courtney took it with a thank-you before turning back to Hannah.

"I'm glad your employee is pleased, but I'm sorry the changes are so late coming. I'm new to the role, and…well, there are many things that I wish had been done long before I took over."

"You can't do anything about that, though," Hannah said. "All you can do is take responsibility now."

"Yes, you're right." Courtney pushed her hair behind her ears, but it was so straight and sleek that it slid right back to where it had been. "I appreciate you telling me about your employee's experience. Hearing comments like that help me to stay the course."

Hannah recalled the time she'd been around Lawrence and how angrily he had spoken to Courtney—his own daughter—during their dinner at the Hot Spot. Hannah imagined that all the tenants appreciated the changes Courtney was making, but even so, it could be very taxing to take a different path than what a parent wanted.

Hannah searched for something encouraging to say. "You're doing important work. And hopefully your dad will see that. He's probably just struggling to let go of what he's built."

Courtney's eyes widened behind her glasses, but then she chuckled. "He definitely is. Sorry, I'd forgotten how these things get around in a small town."

"Oh, I'm sorry." Heat rose to Hannah's cheeks. "I didn't mean to overstep—"

"Nothing to apologize for. I grew up in Blackberry Valley, so it doesn't bother me. I've just been away long enough that I'd forgotten it's impossible to be anonymous here." Courtney fiddled with the straw on her iced coffee. "Yes, Dad has been reluctant to let go, even though the plan has always been for me to take over Lawrence Underhill Properties. And it's not like I'm clueless. I worked in property management for several companies in Atlanta, always knowing that I would someday come back here and take over the family business. But with the way Dad acts now, you'd never know this has always been the plan. You'd think I performed a hostile takeover or something."

"That must be so frustrating," Hannah commiserated.

Courtney cast a bashful look at Hannah. "I'm sorry if I'm oversharing. You asked a simple question, and I just prattled on."

"Not at all," Hannah said. In truth, it was nice to have the distraction from her own problems. "I'm happy to listen. And town gossip wasn't the reason I knew. It was because I saw you at dinner with him last week at the Hot Spot when he got frustrated and left."

Courtney shook her head. "My dad is used to getting his own way, and of course Lincoln always blindly follows whatever Dad wants, as Edward did when he worked for us. I'm the only one around who pushes back when I don't like the way something is being done, and you saw how well it goes for me when I do."

"Not an easy role to be in."

"No." Courtney's laugh sounded self-deprecating. "As evidenced by the fact that I'm standing here in a coffeehouse talking your ear off about it. I'm sorry, Hannah."

"You have nothing to apologize for." Hannah hoped her sincerity was obvious to Courtney. "I've been consumed with my own worries recently, and it's actually nice to talk about something that isn't my fault or responsibility."

"I certainly understand that. Shall we take a seat, and you can tell me about your problems?" Courtney winked. "That seems like a fair trade to me."

Hannah knew Courtney was joking, but also believed the offer was sincere. That if she said she *would* like to talk about her problems, Courtney would let her do exactly that. The offer was made even more tempting by Courtney's association with both Lake brothers. Maybe if Hannah told Courtney everything that was happening at the Hot Spot, then Courtney could talk to Edward and—

No. She wasn't going to twist this pleasant moment of connection into some plea for help from the city.

"It's just some work stuff I'm trying to sort out," Hannah said. "There are things I love about running a restaurant, and there are things that I don't love as much."

"That makes sense." Courtney took a long sip of her coffee. "Most days, I think I must be out of my mind, imagining that I can make a difference at Lawrence Underhill Properties, that I can help my dad see there's more to this business than making money. I can't tell if I'm getting through to him at all, but at the end of the day, taking over the business still feels like what I'm meant to do."

What a remarkable woman, and how fortunate that Hannah had decided to come to Jump Start instead of staying in her office.

"I don't know if you're making progress with your dad or not, but I know you're making a difference in Raquel's life. I'm sure she's not the only one."

"Thank you." Courtney gestured to Hannah's laptop. "I'll stop chatting your ear off now. I know you came here to work. And I better do the same, because I'm supposed to head to Louisville in an hour."

"I really enjoyed talking to you," Hannah said. "We'll have to do it again sometime."

"Absolutely." Courtney drifted toward her own table, which was two away from Hannah's. "You'll be seeing plenty of me, because I can't stay away from the Hot Spot for too long."

Hannah's stomach clenched. She should say something, shouldn't she? This wasn't her trying to use Courtney's contacts, but informing an enthusiastic supporter as to why she wouldn't be able to dine at the Hot Spot for the foreseeable future.

"We're actually having to close for a few days," Hannah said as she moved toward her own table. She kept her voice light. "We have to get a grease trap installed."

"A what?"

"A grease trap. Restaurant kitchens generate a lot of grease, and the trap keeps it out of the city water supply." Hannah opened her laptop and tapped in her password so she wouldn't have to look at Courtney as she explained. "Originally, we were told we didn't need one because of the historic qualities of our building, but apparently the city has changed their minds. We found out yesterday that we'll have to close until we can get one installed."

"How long will that take?"

"I'm not sure yet."

Courtney peered at Hannah over the top of her laptop, lines forming across her forehead. "How frustrating. We deal with similar situations in our business when building codes are updated.

Usually, we have a grace period to make the changes. Were you not given one?"

"I spoke to Edward Lake last night," Hannah said. "He said he would look into it for me."

Courtney's face brightened. "Then it's as good as done. Edward has so much sway in the city. Dad was sorry to lose him from the company, but he'd always known Edward had political aspirations. And it *is* handy in our line of work to know someone in that arena. Edward will have you reopened in no time, I'm sure. He loves the Hot Spot."

Courtney's confidence was contagious, and Hannah felt lighter already. "Yes," she said. "I'm sure you're right. This is just a minor inconvenience, and we'll get it sorted out in no time."

"If not," Courtney said. "You let me know. I'll see what I can do."

Hannah smiled at her new friend. "Thank you. That means more than I can express."

Courtney's phone vibrated, and she adjusted her glasses to read her screen. "I need to take this. Excuse me."

Hannah nodded and focused her attention on her computer. There was a lightness in her heart that she hadn't felt since being dismissed from the city office yesterday afternoon. Because she hadn't been able to make an appointment with Edward until Monday, she'd assumed that she wouldn't hear from him today either, but maybe that was wrong? Maybe Edward worked from home on Fridays or just didn't take meetings on some days of the week. She wouldn't give up hope that the Hot Spot could be open this evening.

Her thoughts turned back to what Courtney had said, about a grace period when building codes changed, which was similar to Liam's question this morning. If only she'd thought to ask Edward for one when they'd been on the phone last night. At the time, she had been too stuck on the fact that she'd originally been told she didn't need a grease trap, and she hadn't been thinking yet about ways to comply with the city as well as keep her business open in the meantime.

But she didn't need to wait for Edward to call her, did she? Hannah unlocked her phone and retrieved the contact information she'd sent herself last night from Aunt Fiona's phone. She hesitated only a moment before pressing the phone icon.

Her call went to voicemail without ringing. While Jump Start wasn't exactly quiet, with its whirring grinders and music, it wasn't loud enough for Hannah to leave a message without others overhearing. She hung up while Edward's recorded voice was still speaking. She'd try again later. At the moment she needed to focus on the work she had come to do.

Working on the website felt much easier now that Hannah had higher hopes about reopening the restaurant. She was immersed in revising the *About the Hot Spot* page when she saw Colt approaching her table, coffee in hand. In his shorts and T-shirt, he looked even younger than usual.

"Hi." She reached for her drink, which she'd neglected for the last fifteen minutes. "How are you?"

"I don't want to bother you." He gestured to her computer. "I just wanted to say how sorry I was about the Hot Spot closing. I saw the post last night."

Hannah leaned back in her chair and stretched her shoulders and neck. "It was an unpleasant surprise for us all."

"If you don't mind me asking, what's the problem?"

Hannah explained once again about grease traps, concluding with, "But I've been talking to the city, and I'm hopeful we won't have to close for as long as we initially feared."

"That's great." Colt drummed his fingers on her table for a moment. "With everything else you have going on, I don't know that you're still interested in that fire, but I went back to the archives again last night. I still can't find the file."

Indeed, Hannah had forgotten about the missing file amid the storm of events that happened yesterday afternoon. "Oh, okay. Thanks for checking again, Colt. I really appreciate it."

He sipped his coffee, eyes unfocused as he appeared to consider something. "I just don't understand why it wouldn't be there. Why would someone remove a file about a fire from the Fourth of July in 1986?"

Hannah leaned back in her seat so she could look up at him easier. "You think someone took it?"

Colt shrugged. "Well, maybe not. But it seems the most likely explanation to me. I mean, we know the fire happened. All other fires have files. Why not this one?"

Hannah frowned. "Maybe someone is trying to hide something?"

"Possibly. Could have also been carelessness, I suppose. But it seems more likely to me that there was something in that file that someone didn't want anybody else to see."

Hannah considered this for a moment, then sighed. "If so, I suppose they got what they wanted. Thanks for trying again."

"Sorry I wasn't able to be more helpful."

"You can't find something that's not there, Colt."

He clapped a hand on her shoulder. "I'll let you get back to work. Good to see you."

After Colt walked away, Hannah tried to focus on her computer. But even while she stared at her screen, her thoughts were on the file. Was Colt's explanation the most likely? Not that the file had been misplaced or was stuck to another, but rather had been purposefully removed?

"Hannah?"

She looked up to find Courtney speaking to her.

"I didn't mean to eavesdrop, but I couldn't help overhearing your conversation. Were you talking about the fire that happened at 5522 Blackbird Road? Fourth of July, 1986?"

"I don't know the exact address, but yes, it was Blackbird Road, and it happened on that date." Hannah remembered now how yesterday afternoon she'd seen Courtney pace along the deck of the big house that had been built on the property. "It used to be a rental house that my friend Theo and his mother lived in."

"Yes, that's the one." Courtney seemed to hesitate. "If you're looking for more information, I may be able to help you."

Chapter Nineteen

Hannah carried her coffee to join Courtney, because this didn't seem like a conversation that should happen while they were seated at different tables. "Do you remember the fire?"

Courtney nodded, her hair swishing slightly. "I was ten. I remember it was quite the finale to the town party."

"Would you mind telling me what you remember?"

Courtney tilted her head to the side, studying Hannah. "Would you mind telling me why you're interested in it?"

That was a fair question. "Theo, the boy who lived at the house, was a childhood friend of my aunt's. The fire caused Theo and his mom to move away, which destroyed his friendship with my aunt. But they've recently reconnected, so the fire has been discussed quite a bit lately."

Hannah considered saying more—about the note and compass she'd found in her apartment, or the guilt both Theo and his mom carried from the night—but she decided against it. Courtney seemed satisfied with the explanation Hannah had given, and that was what mattered right now.

"Like I said, I was ten. We were all watching the town fireworks display, and I was with my best friend and her teenage sister." Courtney smirked. "Her sister was being really sulky because her boyfriend wasn't there. He'd left to shoot off fireworks of his own, and she just kept sighing and making the biggest fuss over it. My friend and I both thought she was being ridiculous. At ten, I still thought boys had cooties."

Courtney chuckled at the memory and Hannah did too, though it was hard to picture Courtney—with her business suits and sleek hair—as a child.

"When we saw other friends from school, we moved over by them just to get away from her sister." Courtney's face lost its amused expression. "But then it became obvious something serious was going on."

"How so?"

"A lot of the adults were distracted and talking to each other. A few were leaving, even though fireworks were still going off. And then the city ended the show abruptly. All the firemen on duty were needed out at Lake Blackberry because of the fire."

Hannah shivered. Only a few weeks ago, she'd attended Blackberry Valley's Fourth of July celebration, and it wasn't hard to imagine how quickly the tone of the party must have changed.

"Wow," Hannah said. "I bet that felt really scary."

Courtney nodded. "I wasn't too scared until I realized my dad was one of the men who had gone. I stayed awake for a long time that night, imagining he was there fighting the fire. He wasn't, of course. He was there because the house belonged to him."

Hannah sipped her coffee. "Did your dad ever say what caused the fire?"

Courtney leaned forward on her elbows. "I probably asked him at some point. It seemed like a natural question. But I don't remember what he said. I know he's always felt the fire was a good thing for our family."

A *good* thing? "Do you mind explaining that?"

Courtney's mouth momentarily pressed into a line. "It feels a bit uncouth to talk about profiting from a tragedy. But with the money from the insurance company, Dad bought more property around the lake. When the county announced they were going to invest in Lake Blackberry and develop the park and recreation area, that property tripled in value. That doesn't happen too often with investments in such a short amount of time."

"Certainly not."

"I think when he bought the extra property, he did so with the intention of building a family home out there. I'm not sure why else he would've wanted it." Courtney shifted in her seat. Her discomfort was obvious. "We never talked about it much. The fire was a terrible tragedy, and we wouldn't have wished that on anyone."

"Of course you wouldn't have wished that on them," Hannah said. "I think that goes without saying."

Courtney's smile was more like a grimace. "Even so, I feel like I should say it. I didn't know who lived there before us, but I did think about them from time to time. I felt bad that the fire cost them everything. Especially since it led to such prosperity for my family."

"That's not your fault."

"I know. I was just a kid. At the time, I was more upset over the Fourth of July party being ruined than anything else. One minute we were celebrating, and the next the town was in crisis."

The sentiment seemed familiar, and it took Hannah a second to realize why. "How funny. I think that's similar to the way both Theo and Edward described their feelings about the evening."

Courtney barked a surprised laugh. "Edward said that? How would he know? He wasn't even there."

Hannah thought back to her conversation with Edward. "Are you sure? He said he was."

"No. He wasn't there for a single second of that party. Remember my friend's older sister's boyfriend? The one she was so mad at because he wasn't watching fireworks with her? Her boyfriend was Edward Lake."

Was Hannah remembering the conversation wrong? She didn't think so. "But that doesn't mean he wasn't there at all, just that he wasn't watching fireworks with his girlfriend. Couldn't he have been elsewhere at the park?"

Courtney's head tilted as she considered this. "Technically, yes. But he and Lincoln had sneaked some fireworks from the city supply. They were gone, shooting them off somewhere."

"How do you know that?"

"Because I saw them." Courtney rattled the ice in her cup, then took a drink of her remaining coffee. "I mean, I didn't see them shooting off the fireworks, but I saw them take the fireworks and leave. My dad was one of the sponsors of the fireworks display—or Lawrence Underhill Properties was a sponsor, I should say. I went with him to pick up the fireworks and bring them to the park before everything got started. Edward and Lincoln happened to be nearby when we arrived, and Dad recruited them to help unload. He sent me off to play on the playground, but that didn't keep me from seeing Edward's and Lincoln's sticky fingers when Dad wasn't looking."

Hannah let this information soak in. "Hasn't that always been one of the theories about how the house burned down? That it might've been a forgotten appliance, but it also might have been an errant firework?"

"Yes." Courtney dragged out the syllable. "But I didn't mean to suggest that Edward or Lincoln might be involved. You have to remember that Lake Blackberry wasn't then what it is now. Driving all the way out there just to shoot off a few fireworks seems like an odd choice."

"I guess," Hannah said, but she wasn't quite ready to dismiss the idea that Edward and Lincoln might've set Theo's house on fire. Inadvertently, of course.

"Anyway." Courtney straightened. "The reason I thought I might be able to help you is that I'm guessing we have a file on that fire at the office."

Hannah felt her heart rate pick up. "You think so?"

"I think it's possible." Courtney tapped her manicured fingernail against the tabletop. "In the eighties and nineties, my dad had a meticulously organized secretary named Minnie who had an elaborate filing system. That fire would've been an insurance claim, so Minnie would've filed every document, and perhaps even gone so far as to request a copy of the file from the fire department just to have a set for our records too. She was thorough like that."

Hannah leaned forward, unable to keep the enthusiasm out of her voice as she asked, "Do you mind looking? I know you're very busy, and I hate to impose on your time, but it would mean a lot to Theo and his mom."

"I'll see what I can do." Courtney's smartwatch buzzed on her wrist. "That's my reminder to pack up and leave. I have several meetings in Louisville this afternoon. But I'll be back at the office tomorrow and could look at our files then."

"That would be great," Hannah said. "And I'm happy to help, if you'd like."

"Sure." Courtney smiled. "I could meet you at the office tomorrow after one?'

"That works for me."

They exchanged numbers, and Courtney gave Hannah the address of the Lawrence Underhill Properties offices.

"Hopefully we'll be alone and won't have to explain ourselves." Courtney slid her laptop into a protective case. "If we do encounter Lincoln or Dad, I'll have to come up with some kind of story."

Hannah nodded. "I'm sure they wouldn't want a stranger poking around in their files."

"Well, yes, that's part of it, but also they're just..." Courtney trailed off. "I don't want to give the wrong impression. Both Dad and Lincoln are capable of great kindness, but if either of them feels threatened or backed into a corner, watch out."

Hannah frowned, unsure of how to respond. Finally, she settled on, "I suppose that's true for most of us."

"Sure. Not like them, though. Actually, Edward is the worst offender of the three, in my opinion." Courtney fit her leather bag over her shoulder but remained seated. She lowered her voice. "A few years ago, his ex-wife tried to open a boutique in Blackberry Valley. The amount of red tape that popped up was ridiculous. Licenses, construction permits, city inspectors. On and on. The poor woman finally gave up and opened her store elsewhere."

The back of Hannah's neck prickled as she thought of the Open sign on her restaurant that had remained off all last night. A sudden need for a grease trap didn't sound too different from the situation Courtney was describing between Edward and his ex-wife.

But that was silly. Why would Edward target Hannah? She barely even knew the man.

"I thought his behavior was ghastly," Courtney continued as she stood. "But both Dad and Lincoln laughed when they told me about it. Like it was some big joke."

"What happened to his ex-wife?"

"Oh." Courtney grinned. "Well, this is where the joke is on Edward, I guess. I know her life felt rough for a bit, but by all outward appearances, she's thriving now. Her boutique is doing great—from what I can tell on social media, anyway—and she married a man who owns the restaurant next door. God is amazing like that, isn't He? Redirecting our paths when they need it. It doesn't always feel good in the moment, but He takes care of us, doesn't He?"

Hannah felt a smile spread across her face. "He really does."

"I'll be late if I don't leave now." Courtney pushed her chair back under the table. "But I'll see you tomorrow."

Hannah returned to her own table, where her laptop had gone to sleep. She sure didn't understand what God was up to right now, but she was thankful for the chance to connect with Courtney. And she trusted that, regardless of what happened next, He would take care of her.

Chapter Twenty

"But why would Edward target the Hot Spot like that?" Lacy asked as she tossed a handful of chicken feed across the yard. The chickens raced after it, clucking and pecking with gusto. "It doesn't make sense."

After Hannah finally admitted to herself that her heart wasn't really in doing website work today, she'd left Jump Start and driven to Bluegrass Hollow Farm. She hoped Lacy was available for a chat or needed help around the farm so she could get her mind off things.

Hannah had found her best friend in a loose-fitting, sky-blue maternity dress, taking care of her beloved chickens. With a bandanna secured over her reddish-brown hair, Lacy was a vision from a bygone era.

"I don't know," Hannah said. "Other than last night when I interrupted his golf game, the vast majority of our conversations have been related to food and what he was going to order off the menu."

Lacy frowned and lowered herself into a folding chair. There wasn't always a folding chair out there, but over the last few months, more and more had appeared in different locations around Bluegrass Hollow Farm.

"I mean, the ketchup bottle at his table *was* empty the other night," Hannah said in an attempt to lighten the mood. "Could be that."

Lacy nodded with mock gravity. "Some people are very serious about their condiments. Especially ketchup people."

Hannah grinned. "And then I embarrassed myself in front of him because Colt and I were talking about the fire. Edward asked if looking up old fires was a hobby of mine."

Lacy snorted a laugh and threw out another handful of feed to the chickens. "Did you say, 'Yes. That and perusing old high school yearbooks'?"

"It was really awkward." Hannah laughed just from the memory of Edward's baffled expression. "I used Liam as an excuse. Like because we're getting married, I need to know stuff about major fires that happened in town."

"So smooth."

"That's me."

Lacy shifted in the chair and crossed her ankles. "Did Edward say anything about the fire, or just ask why you cared?"

"He did say a few things." Hannah tipped her face up to the sky as she thought about it. "That it was a tragedy. That he'd heard Theo's mom started it. He said that he was at the town's Fourth of July party, and it was really awful how quickly everything went from celebration to crisis." Hannah frowned and lowered herself to the grass beside Lacy's chair. "But that's actually a strange inconsistency. When I mentioned that to Courtney, she said that Edward wasn't there."

Lacy drained the last from the water bottle that she carried with her constantly these days. "How can she be sure, though? It's a huge party every year. Half the time I can't find Neil in that crowd."

"Is it because he's actually reading, back at Legend & Key?"

Lacy grinned. "No, but I've definitely checked before."

Hannah laughed. It would be just like Neil to slip away from a town party in favor of a cozy armchair and a good book or an antique map. "Courtney says she remembers because her best friend's older sister was dating Edward at the time, and the sister was upset that he wasn't there. Courtney says she saw Edward and Lincoln steal fireworks, but she thinks it's unlikely that it would be connected to the fire at Theo's house. She thinks Lake Blackberry would've been out of the way for them just to shoot off a few fireworks."

"Huh." Lacy slumped back into her chair. "Well, I might be missing something, but nothing in the conversation that you had with Edward makes it sound like he felt threatened and decided he had better shut down your restaurant and run you out of town. Aside from the empty ketchup bottle, of course."

"I know," Hannah said with a sigh. "I just thought it might mean something when Courtney told me about what happened with his ex-wife."

"Yeah, me too, but I don't see how him shutting you down accomplishes anything meaningful. I assume the situation with his ex-wife was about revenge or pettiness, neither of which applies in this situation."

"Agreed. All I know is that I want my restaurant to be reopened." Hannah looked at her phone. Nearly two o'clock, and still she'd heard nothing from Edward. "Maybe I'll try calling him again. I've already left two voicemails asking about a window of compliance. Maybe I need to leave a third."

"Seems sensible to me," Lacy said.

They sat together in companionable silence for a bit, watching the chickens peck at the ground. The afternoon was warm without much of a breeze, and even though she was just sitting there, Hannah felt sweat trickle down her back.

"Do you have more to do out here, or are you ready to go inside?" she asked.

"I've been ready to go inside for a bit," Lacy said, "but that means having to stand up and walk all the way to the house."

Hannah smiled at her friend and got to her feet. "Good thing I'm here to help you."

"I can always count on you." Lacy leaned forward and then pushed herself to her feet. "How are things with your aunt and Theo?"

"Good, I think," Hannah said as they shuffled along the path to the Minyards' house. "They're really sweet together."

"Wouldn't it be so romantic if they ended up married after all these years?" Lacy clasped her hands together. "Like something from a movie."

"Aunt Fiona is always very quick to say they're just friends. However, when we were paddleboarding yesterday, I learned that Theo's mom is coming to Blackberry Valley this weekend with the express purpose of seeing Aunt Fiona."

Lacy gasped. "What? That seems like a serious step."

"I know, right?"

Hannah's smile wavered. When Theo had mentioned this, Hannah had imagined the three of them—Aunt Fiona, Theo, and Theo's mom—sitting in the Hot Spot together, where Hannah could spoil them with extra appetizers and observe their interactions. That wasn't going to happen now.

"You sighed," Lacy said.

"Did I? I was thinking about the Hot Spot. I think I'll try calling Edward again. I won't leave another voicemail, but if I don't hear from him soon, there's zero chance of us getting the restaurant open tomorrow, much less tonight."

"Great idea. If you think it will sway his opinion at all, tell him that I need the Hot Spot open because I'm craving a fried chicken salad. Ooh, and pizza. Pizza sounds good. If you're not open tonight, I think I'll get pizza. But I'd rather have that salad, so let Edward know."

Hannah laughed. "I'm sure your cravings will be what convinces him."

"Never come between a pregnant lady and her cravings." Lacy opened her back door and gave a dramatic "Ahh" as the cool air rushed to greet them. "Are you coming inside?"

"No, I better get going. Thanks for stopping and talking to me, though."

"I wish I could do more than that," Lacy said. "I wish I could snap my fingers and make all of this go away."

"Me too," Hannah said with a grin. "That would be so handy."

Hannah gave Lacy a swift hug goodbye and then headed out to her car, where she cranked the air conditioner to full blast. While nothing in her situation had really changed during the time she'd spent at Lacy's, she still felt lighter as she drove back home.

The heaviness returned, however, when she called Edward yet again, only to reach the now-familiar recording of his voice inviting her to leave a message.

Saturday morning, Hannah awoke to a message from her aunt asking her to call. The message had been sent several hours ago—Aunt Fiona hadn't been joking about being an early riser—and Hannah hurriedly punched the button to do as her aunt requested. Maybe Aunt Fiona had spoken with Edward, and Hannah would finally be able to open the Hot Spot.

"Good morning," Aunt Fiona answered. "If it really *is* still morning."

Hannah chuckled. "It's eight thirty. That's a perfectly respectable time to be starting the day."

"Okay, okay," Aunt Fiona said. "And I guess I shouldn't harass you when I'm calling to ask a favor, should I?"

Hannah's heart sank. Not that she minded helping her aunt with something, but "a favor" meant Aunt Fiona hadn't magically fixed her restaurant problem. "What's going on?"

"I've been meaning to visit your mother's grave ever since I got back to town, but I've put it off because—well, I want to go, and I also don't want to go." There was a slight pause. "Do you know what I mean?"

When Hannah moved back to Blackberry Valley, she'd gone to visit the cemetery where her mother and grandparents were buried, but it wasn't something she made a habit of. When she wanted to feel connected to her mother, she was much more likely to go home, where happy memories of Frieda Prentiss abounded.

"I know exactly what you mean," Hannah said. "And I'd be happy to visit with you."

"It really doesn't bother you?"

"No, not at all. When would you like to go?"

"This morning, if it's not too inconvenient for you. Theo and his mom are going to be in town in time for lunch—for which we'd love to have you join us—so I wanted to be done before it was time to meet them."

"Sure, that sounds easy enough." Hannah yawned and stared at her burbling coffeepot. "I just woke up, so I need some time. But I could probably pick you up around nine thirty?"

"That would be perfect." Aunt Fiona sounded relieved, as though Hannah were doing her an enormous favor. "Thank you, Hannah."

It was closer to nine forty-five when Hannah rolled into her dad's driveway, but Aunt Fiona didn't seem bothered by her tardiness. She emerged from the house, lovely in a lavender dress with a scalloped hem, and holding three small bouquets of daisies.

"That color always makes me think of Mom," Hannah said while Aunt Fiona buckled her seat belt.

Her aunt smiled. "Me too. That's actually why I bought this dress."

The cemetery wasn't very far outside of town, and Aunt Fiona was quiet for the entire drive. Hannah tried a few times to get conversation going before deciding her aunt must not want that. She let her sit quietly with her thoughts.

Soon, they pulled through the cemetery gates, which were ornamental rather than a means for securing anything, because there was no fence around the grounds. On one end of the cemetery a burial ceremony was underway, but her mom's grave was on the opposite side, so they wouldn't disturb the other mourners. Hannah led Aunt Fiona along the path to where her grandparents and her mother were buried.

When they arrived at the graves, Hannah lingered near the walking trail while Aunt Fiona drew close to the markers. She placed two bouquets on the marker for her parents and said a few words that Hannah couldn't hear.

Then she moved down the row to where her sister was buried. Here Aunt Fiona stood for an extended time. Hannah had resolved to let her have her moment without interfering, but then her aunt began wiping her eyes repeatedly. Hannah couldn't allow her to stand there crying without drawing close and putting an arm around her.

Aunt Fiona leaned against Hannah's shoulder, quietly weeping. "I miss Frieda so much. It doesn't seem fair to have lost her so early."

"I know," Hannah said. "I feel the same way. Though she probably would've said to me, 'Hannah, who said anything about life being fair?'"

Aunt Fiona gave a watery laugh and dabbed her eyes with a tissue. "That's exactly what she would've said. It used to make me crazy, and now I would pay everything in my bank account just to hear her say that again."

Hannah thought of times throughout childhood when she'd grumbled about Mom. Times when Mom made her do things around the house that seemed completely unfair from her teenage perspective, like having to clean the bathroom before she went out to the movies, or being required to make her bed before friends came over. Hannah's complaints all sounded silly now, and like her aunt, she would pay a lot of money to have her mom scold her for leaving her bed unmade.

"I think one of the reasons I've stayed away from Blackberry Valley so long is because of Frieda," Aunt Fiona said in a voice tight with tears. "When I'm away from here, there's so little that reminds me of her. Sure, I'll see a woman with the same shade of hair and think of her, or a song will come on that she and I used to sing along to in the car. But it's not like being home. When I'm here, it sometimes feels like I'm drowning in memories."

Hannah nodded along. "I understand that completely. When I moved back from Los Angeles, the grief of having lost Mom felt so fresh again."

"I wish I'd been brave enough to come visit more." Aunt Fiona twisted the tissue clutched in her hands. "I missed out on a lot because I didn't want to accept how life had changed. Yes, it means that I didn't have to feel the grief of losing my sister as acutely, but it also means I missed out on happy moments with you. With Drew and Allison and the kids."

Hannah squeezed her aunt's shoulders one more time and then released her. "Don't be too hard on yourself."

Aunt Fiona wiped her eyes once more. "Here I've been so angry with Theo for so long when I've basically been doing the same thing. Avoiding Blackberry Valley. Avoiding the loss that happened here."

Hannah could see her aunt's perspective, but couldn't resist pointing out, "They're two very different situations, Aunt Fiona."

"Yes, you're right." Aunt Fiona nodded. "He was only sixteen and didn't know any better, while I was in my late forties and *did* know better."

Hannah chuckled softly. "That's not what I meant, and you know it."

Aunt Fiona offered her a ghost of a smile. "Change has always been very hard on me. Especially change I have no control over, like Theo leaving or your mom dying. My life isn't at all what I dreamed it would be when I was in high school and planning my future, but the Lord has always been so good to me. He takes care of me no matter what."

Hannah considered this. She'd also been wrestling with change recently. With what the arrival of the Minyards' baby would mean for her relationship with Lacy, or what her life would look like after her marriage to Liam. These were good changes that she was excited for—that she'd prayed for—but also there were unknowns that left her feeling anxious.

And that fear of change was even more true when, like her aunt said, the change wasn't something Hannah had chosen, like a city code changing and shutting down her restaurant. A change that could cost her thousands of dollars. *I don't know what to do here, God. I don't know how to make this situation better. But I trust You.*

"You hummed," Aunt Fiona said. "Was that a sound of agreement?"

"Yes, it was. I was thinking about what you just said and how hard it can feel to see the good in what happened or how God is going to use it."

Aunt Fiona nodded. "And sometimes we don't see it until years later, in my experience. But time and time again, I come back to my favorite Proverb. 'Trust in the Lord with all your heart and lean not on your own understanding; in all your ways, submit to Him, and He will make your paths straight.'"

"I could use a straight path right now," Hannah said with a weary sigh. "Because I definitely do *not* understand the turn of events with my restaurant, and I'm out of ideas for what to do next."

Aunt Fiona wrapped an arm around Hannah's shoulders. "Me neither. We will trust in the Lord together."

When Aunt Fiona reiterated her invitation to Hannah to join her, Theo, and Theo's mom, Ivy, for pizza, Hannah gladly accepted. She was excited to meet the woman she'd heard so much about.

"I have an appointment at one," Hannah said as she pulled into the busy parking lot of the pizza place. "Will Theo be able to get you back to Dad's house if I need to go to my meeting straight from here?"

"Yes, that won't be a problem," Aunt Fiona said as she studied her reflection in the passenger mirror. "The last hour really did a number on my eye makeup, didn't it?"

"Understandably so."

Hannah considered mentioning to her aunt that her appointment was with Lawrence Underhill's daughter. That they'd be searching for a file that might shed light on what had caused the fire. But Aunt Fiona grabbed her purse and popped open the passenger door. This didn't seem like an ideal time to spring that news on her, and there wasn't a point in getting her aunt's hopes up when Courtney wasn't even sure that such a file existed.

Hannah locked her car and followed her aunt into the restaurant. She loved walking into pizzerias, where the strong scents of yeasty dough and Parmesan cheese enveloped her. She was still inhaling deeply and savoring the moment when Aunt Fiona tugged at her arm.

"They're already seated."

Aunt Fiona pointed to where Theo and his mom were in a red vinyl booth beside the window, grinning with identical smiles. Theo's mom stood as soon as she spotted Aunt Fiona. Ivy couldn't have been more than five feet tall and had a similar olive complexion to Theo's, with silver waves of hair that fell just below her chin.

"Fiona Western," she said in a voice that was deeper than Hannah had expected. "You're as darling as you were in high school."

Aunt Fiona laughed and flushed red. "I'm not so sure about that, Ivy, but it is so good to see you again."

The two women hugged. Hannah glanced at Theo, who watched his mom and Aunt Fiona with an expression of pure delight.

When they released each other, Aunt Fiona tugged Hannah forward. "This is my niece, Hannah."

Hannah held out a hand to the woman. "So nice to meet you, Mrs. Drakos."

"Please call me Ivy." Her eyes crinkled at the corners as she smiled up at Hannah. "I can see your grandmother in your features. She was such a wonderful woman."

"She was, yes."

Ivy's smile flickered. "I was sorry to hear she passed a few years ago. Maybe I should expect that more at my age, but I forget how old I am half the time."

"I certainly understand that," Aunt Fiona said as she slid into the booth across from Theo. Hannah scooted in after her aunt. "These new nurses arrive at the hospital looking like babies and I think, 'Surely I was older when I started working.'"

Ivy resumed her seat. "Theo tells me you've made quite a life for yourself as a nurse, traveling all over the country."

Aunt Fiona blushed. "I think he's overselling me, but I *am* a nurse, and I have lived in a number of places."

Theo arched his eyebrows. "I'm not overselling you."

Aunt Fiona's cheeks grew even redder.

The server materialized at the table with his order pad in hand and an expectant look on his face.

"Sorry," Hannah told him. "We haven't even touched the menus yet. Could you give us a few minutes?"

"Of course," the young man said, though his smile didn't quite mask his irritation.

Hannah understood the lunch hour was a busy time, but she would've been horrified if Raquel or Dylan treated a customer in such a way. Even so, after he left, Hannah took charge of finding out what everyone liked on their pizza, so they could place their order when he returned. Hannah had barely finished calculating how much pizza they needed to order when the server reappeared.

As soon as he'd written down the order and left, Theo said to his mom, "You know the old fire station in town? Hannah has renovated it and turned it into an amazing restaurant."

"Really?" Ivy looked at Hannah. "Why aren't we eating there, then?"

Aunt Fiona inhaled sharply, but Hannah managed a smile. "We don't serve lunch."

"I'll stay in town through dinner, then, and you can take me." Ivy patted her son's shoulder. Then she grinned at Hannah. "Unless you're closed on Saturdays, of course."

She was obviously joking, and Hannah wished she could laugh. She felt a zip of frustration that she still hadn't heard back from Edward Lake. She had a hard time imagining that he would call her on a Saturday, which meant the Hot Spot wouldn't open at all this weekend. Hannah tried not to let her thoughts stray to her employees' lost wages and her own lost revenue.

"Not typically, though we are closed today, oddly." Hannah attempted a smile. "We had to close unexpectedly for a few days to update some equipment."

"Well, that's unfortunate timing." Ivy lifted her glass of ice water to her mouth. "I would've loved to have eaten there. Maybe next time I'm in town?"

"I'll save a special table for you," Hannah promised.

"When Theo was a boy, there was a fireman who worked at that station by the name of Kenneth Cutuli. Do you know him?"

"Only by reputation," Hannah said. "He sounds like he was quite an amazing man."

"He was. And his wife, Joan, was a gem too. Not all the women were as welcoming as she was." Ivy's smile was tinged with sadness. "I understand. I'm a bit of an oddball."

"Mom, don't talk about yourself like that," Theo scolded.

"It's true, though. And I was shy and withdrawn at the time. I didn't find my confidence until I took up pottery."

Hannah didn't know how one affected the other, but there wasn't time to ask because Ivy pressed on.

"Joan and I exchanged letters for a little while after we moved, but eventually we lost touch. It was nobody's fault, just one of those things that happens over time. Especially in those days. We didn't have email, and long-distance calls were so expensive. Anyway, we had..." Ivy swallowed hard and fiddled with the paper ring from her silverware roll. "Something terrible happened to us—"

"She knows about the fire," Theo said in a gentle voice.

"Oh." Ivy grimaced. "Yes, well, Joan and Kenneth took us in right after that happened. Even though it was my fault."

"Mom." Theo's syllable somehow was both sharp and full of love.

Ivy patted her son's hand. "I know, honey, but it's time I stop shying away from talking about it. That's one of the reasons why I wanted to come back here and see the town. Maybe I'll never be able to forgive myself for what happened, but I want to try. Spending the last forty years avoiding the subject and not talking about it hasn't helped me to move on, so I'm trying a different approach."

"That's very admirable, Ivy," Aunt Fiona said, "but the last I heard, it still wasn't a stated fact that you're responsible for what happened at the house."

Ivy laced her hands together on top of the table. "I've always been terribly forgetful. I baked a pie that afternoon for the Fourth of July celebration and probably never turned off the oven. I could cry right now thinking of what my forgetfulness cost my son. What it cost you, Fiona."

Theo shifted his weight in his seat. "Mom, you're taking on too much responsibility for what happened."

Ivy unfastened her silverware roll and smoothed the napkin on the wooden table. "In fact I'm so forgetful, I can't even remember why I brought this up in the first place." She punctuated this with a dry laugh.

"Because Hannah has a restaurant in the old fire station, and you were talking about Kenneth and Joan," Theo said.

"That's right." Ivy smiled at her son. "You always keep me on track. Do Kenneth and Joan still live in town? I'd love to see them again."

"They moved to Florida a decade ago, Rusty says," Theo said. "As far as he knows, they're both very much enjoying living near the ocean and their grandchildren."

"That's wonderful to hear. Joan always loved the beach."

The conversation drifted to the topic of old friends and remained there until the pizza arrived. Hannah had just slid a slice onto her plate when her phone vibrated with an incoming call. *Please, Lord, let it be Edward Lake finally calling me back!*

But when she dug the phone out of her purse, Hannah was surprised to see Courtney Underhill's name lighting up her screen. It was still thirty minutes until they were supposed to meet. Maybe she was calling to reschedule?

"Sorry," Hannah said to the others at the table. "This is the woman I have a meeting with at one o'clock, so I'd better take this."

Aunt Fiona shooed her away good-naturedly.

Hannah stepped away and answered the call. "Courtney?"

"Hi, Hannah." Courtney's voice had a slight tremble to it. "I know we're supposed to meet at one, but can you come to Lawrence Underhill Properties now? I've found something that I think you'll be interested in."

Chapter Twenty-One

Hannah rushed across the parking lot to her Subaru, car keys in one hand and a slice of pizza clutched in the other.

"Hannah!"

She turned toward one of her favorite voices and found Lacy's pickup parked several spots down from her own car. Lacy sat behind the wheel, a small pizza box resting on her round stomach.

Hannah couldn't resist giggling. "You look like you're having a very pregnant moment right now."

Lacy grinned and raised the slice she was halfway through eating. "The baby wanted pepperoni. Who am I to argue?" She nodded toward Hannah's Subaru. "I thought that was your car."

Hannah leaned against Lacy's open window. "I was having lunch with Aunt Fiona, Theo, and Theo's mom, but I just got a call from Courtney. We were supposed to meet at one today, but she asked me to come now. Said she found something she thinks I'll want to see."

Hannah had barely finished her sentence when Lacy unbuckled her seat belt. "I'm going with you. I can bring my pizza, right?"

"Of course," Hannah said as Lacy slid out of the truck, pizza box still in hand.

These days, Lacy walked distinctly like a pregnant woman, not that Hannah would ever utter the word *waddle* to her best friend.

Lacy lowered herself into the passenger seat of the Subaru. "This is way better than sitting at home thinking about all the things that need to be done but that I can't physically do right now."

"This worked out great," Hannah agreed, redirecting a few air vents toward Lacy.

Lacy buckled her seat belt. "All right. Step on it!"

Hannah chuckled. She knew it wasn't worth speeding to Lawrence Underhill Properties—it wasn't as though this was a life or death situation—but she had a hard time not pressing her foot harder on the gas pedal as she navigated the Blackberry Valley streets. There wasn't much to say that was new, since Hannah had filled Lacy in on everything while they fed chickens.

Fortunately, the drive was only a few minutes long, and as best friends, they had never had trouble filling silences—or enjoying companionable ones. Hannah slowed the vehicle as Lawrence Underhill Properties came into view.

"I really hope this means she found a file," Lacy said as she polished off the last slice of her personal-size pizza.

Hannah eased the Subaru into the driveway. "I hope so too. I guess we're about to find out."

Lawrence Underhill Properties occupied what had once been a house on the edge of town and over time had become a house surrounded by businesses. It was a lovely two-story home, painted a crisp white with black shutters, and a cheery red door. The wide porch that stretched along the front made Hannah think of evenings in rocking chairs with glasses of sweet tea or lemonade. Had she been visiting under different circumstances, she might've taken more time to admire the home, but instead she parked her car behind Courtney's distinctive yellow Jeep, then she and Lacy hurried to the door.

But at the door, Hannah hesitated before reaching for the doorknob. Doing so felt odd, despite the sign on the front door reading LAWRENCE UNDERHILL PROPERTIES: COME ON IN.

"It does feel a little awkward, doesn't it?" Lacy said, looking up at the house. "A bit like opening the door to a stranger's home."

"I guess that's why they put that sign up," Hannah said. She twisted the knob and pushed.

The interior didn't resemble a home at all, but was appointed as an office, which made it feel easier to walk inside. They stepped into a waiting room, with a receptionist's desk, a coat rack, and several comfortable-looking chairs. Natural light streamed through the windows, but the desk lights and computer were off.

"It's quiet in here," Lacy whispered.

"Courtney?" Hannah called down a hallway, which was decorated with framed photos of famous buildings. "It's Hannah."

"Come on back." Courtney's head popped into view from one of the doorways, her dark hair swinging like a curtain. "Sorry, my office is soundproof. I didn't hear you."

When Courtney's gaze flicked to Lacy, Hannah said, "This is my friend, Lacy. We were at the same place when you called, and we've been working together to understand what happened that night at the fire. I hope it's okay that I brought her."

"I'm like the Dr. Watson to her Sherlock," Lacy said.

Hannah laughed. "She's joking."

Courtney smiled warmly at Lacy. "It's so nice to meet you. I've seen you around town."

Lacy rested both hands on her stomach. "I'm hard to miss these days. This office is lovely."

"Thank you. Let me get a better seat for you, Lacy."

Hannah and Lacy stepped into Courtney's office, which was painted the color of daffodils. The space had minimal furnishings, just a wide cherry desk and a row of sparsely filled shelves. There were a few real estate books and office supplies, but no personal decorations.

Courtney dragged a cushioned chair from the corner and positioned it close to the desk. "Here, Lacy." She shot an apologetic look at Hannah. "I only have one of these, unfortunately."

"That's fine." Hannah perched on a wooden chair. "I'm just glad you had something for Lacy."

"Once upon a time when I wanted to sit, it didn't feel so complicated," Lacy said as she eased herself into the chair. "I'm looking forward to that again. Someday."

Courtney took a seat behind her desk. "I remember that. Or the effort it took to roll over in bed at night. I don't miss those days. When are you due?"

"Middle of August."

Courtney's eyes widened. "Wow. You don't have much longer. Do you have other kids?"

"Nope. This is baby number one."

"That's so exciting," Courtney said. "I love babies."

Hannah's gaze drifted to the manila folder open on Courtney's desk. She tilted her head, trying to read the printed label, which didn't go unnoticed by Courtney.

"I arrived early and started going through the files. It didn't take long to find this." Courtney exhaled loudly through her nose. "I'm having a little trouble making sense of it all, but nothing I've found seems particularly good. Here, take a look."

Dread turned into a hard knot in Hannah's stomach as Courtney handed her a small packet of pages, a typewritten report of the fire. The logo belonged to an insurance company, and the paper had yellowed with time. Hannah held the document angled toward Lacy so they could both read. She skimmed through the verbiage until she reached the cause of the fire.

Hannah touched her finger to the text. "Well, that's interesting."

"I assume you mean the cause of the fire?" Courtney leaned forward in her chair and rested her elbows on her desk. "Or rather, the causes."

Lacy looked up from the report. "So, they think the fire was caused by *both* a gas burner being left on *and* a nearby grass fire started by a firework?"

Courtney shrugged. "That's what the report says."

"What are the odds of both of those things happening simultaneously?" Lacy said.

Courtney's smile turned wry. "A bit too coincidental, don't you think?"

"But surely you don't think Ivy or Theo would've intentionally set fire to their own house?" Hannah asked, the incredulousness she felt clear in her voice. "Because I don't think that's what happened."

"No, not Ivy or Theo." Courtney swallowed hard. "I think…I think maybe my father is involved somehow. Like maybe he accidentally set the house on fire."

Hannah considered this. If so, that would explain why Lawrence had been so surprisingly generous with Ivy and Theo. He would want to minimize questions as much as possible.

"Why do you think that?" Lacy asked.

Courtney set an eight-by-ten photograph on the desk and pushed it across to the women. "Because of this picture."

Hannah took the print by the edges and examined it. The photograph captured the charred remains of a kitchen, which Hannah only recognized as such because of the skeletons of kitchen appliances. Nearly everything else in the photograph was misshapen and blackened to the point of being unrecognizable.

"I think you'll need to help us out," Hannah said. "I'm not seeing anything that points to your dad."

Courtney passed a magnifying glass to them and pointed at the corner of the picture.

Lacy held the magnifying glass where Courtney's shiny fingernail indicated. The object was a slim rectangle. Part of the rectangle was scorched black, but the rest was a silvery color and appeared to have an ornate design on it.

"Is it a lighter?" Hannah guessed.

Courtney nodded.

Lacy frowned. "You think this is how the fire was started?"

"That seems possible. What I know is that my father used to be a smoker, and *that* was his lighter. It was a fixture of my childhood, but he lost it at some point. And I can't think of a single reason it would've been in this house when it burned."

Hannah bit her lower lip, disliking what Courtney implied but also understanding her line of thought. "Unless he'd been there recently."

"Maybe he dropped it when he was inspecting the house after the fire," Hannah suggested.

"That's what I hoped when I first saw it, but I don't think so." Courtney tapped the corner of the photo. "See how it's burned? Seems to me that would only happen if it was inside during the fire."

Silence fell over the room.

Lacy cocked her head. "Do you hear something?"

After a moment, Hannah heard it too: solid, purposeful footsteps in the hallway.

"Hide everything," Courtney whispered, then called out, "Hello?"

Hannah's hands trembled as she scraped the papers together into the folder.

"Courtney?" called a male voice.

"In my office," Courtney called back.

Lincoln materialized in the doorway a moment later. His smile swept over Hannah and Lacy. "Sorry to interrupt, ladies."

"I didn't know you were coming in this afternoon." Courtney pushed several photographs toward Hannah, but in her overexcitement, one shot off the end of the desk and glided to a stop in her office doorway.

Right in front of Lincoln's shiny wingtip shoes. He bent, picked up the photograph, and blanched.

"Just cleaning out some old files," Courtney said in a voice that she probably meant to sound lighthearted and casual. Hannah thought it was too high to be convincing, and that was before Courtney strode across the room and snatched the photo from Lincoln's grasp. "What are you doing here today?"

Instead of replying, he took several steps into the room, his eyes on the closed file. Hannah realized too late that she should've flipped over the folder on the desk, because across the tab was a neatly typed label that read, *7/4/86 Insurance Claim*.

"That's great." Lincoln also spoke in a voice that Hannah thought he intended to sound casual, but it came out tense. "I'm sure those files need cleaning out. Where did you find that?"

"In the filing cabinet," Courtney said.

Lincoln shifted his weight from foot to foot as his gaze flicked between the three of them. Hannah had never seen a man in his fifties appear so young, so vulnerable. "But why are you looking at *that* file?"

Courtney's head tipped to the side. "Lincoln, is there something you'd like to tell us?"

Gone was the smooth businessman Hannah had spoken to at the Hot Spot. Lincoln's breathing was quick and shallow. He stared at Courtney, seemingly incapable of replying.

"What do you think we've found, Lincoln?" Hannah asked in her gentlest voice. "You look worried."

His gaze skittered between the three of them. "Is there a reason you all are looking at this specific file? Because"—he swallowed hard—"it can be really hard to understand nuances of what happened just from reading reports. You might draw some false conclusions when in fact, you don't know. You can't understand. Because you weren't there."

"Lincoln." Courtney's voice was stern. A mother's voice, despite Lincoln being a couple years older than her. "What do you know about that fire?"

He pushed his hands through his gel-sculpted hair and sagged against the wall. His breathing was still fast and shallow. Hannah had never witnessed a panic attack, but Lincoln seemed to be on the cusp of one.

"You don't understand," he rasped, his voice sounding young and frightened. "How could you? We thought we were far enough away from their house. We didn't see any fire, or we never would've left without trying to put it out. Never. We didn't even know what happened until we got back to town and everyone was talking about the fire."

To Hannah, it appeared as though years were falling away from Lincoln's face. He was no longer a successful businessman or a middle-aged father, but a teenager reliving what must have been one of the worst days of his life.

"Those fireworks you and Edward stole from the town supply," Courtney said. "That's what started the fire?"

Lincoln's nod was barely perceptible.

"How could you not have told anyone?" Courtney demanded.

"Because I was fourteen and scared out of my mind," Lincoln said, hands in his hair again. "Edward told me to just keep my mouth shut, so I did. It was an accident." His eyes searched each of their faces, silently pleading for them to understand. "You have to believe me. It was an accident."

"I believe you." Courtney exhaled slowly through her nose. "But Dad deserves to know."

Lincoln's gaze shifted to his feet. "Lawrence does know."

Courtney frowned. "You and Edward told him?"

"Well, kind of. After we got back to town and found out about the fire, Edward and I vowed to stay silent about where we'd been and what we'd been doing. But the next day, your dad knocked on our door. He told us firework debris was found near the scene and demanded to know the truth. He knew we'd had access to the town fireworks, because he'd asked us to help him unload."

"And Dad kept it quiet all these years?" Courtney asked.

Lincoln nodded. Hannah thought he appeared as miserable as if the whole ordeal had just taken place. What a weight this must have been.

"He did. Maybe because he knew our dad had broken his back and was out of work. Or because he knew we'd made a mistake that we couldn't afford. Whatever the reason, Lawrence told us that the fire couldn't be undone, and that he wouldn't tell anyone if we didn't. It felt like such a gift."

"I'm sure it did," Hannah murmured.

And maybe it had been intended as a gift, but one look at Lincoln's face made Hannah think it had actually been a curse. He'd been saddled with this secret, this guilt, all these years.

Lincoln rubbed at his chin. "I hadn't thought about the fire in a long time, but with Theo in town recently, it's all been dredged up again. I can't change what happened in 1986. I can't change that I stayed quiet all these years, but maybe now that I'm older I could do..." His hand fluttered, as if he could pluck the right solution from the air. "Something. The right thing. Whatever that is."

Silence weighed on the room. Hannah searched for words to say that might break the tension without excusing the choices Lincoln had made.

"It wasn't entirely you, though." Lacy reached for the file on Courtney's desk and flipped it open. "The report says that a gas burner had been left on."

"The oven," Hannah corrected.

"No," Courtney said. "The report says a gas burner."

Hannah frowned and leaned forward. Sure enough, the report really did say that the burner had been left on. "That's strange. I thought it was the oven."

"Where did you find that?" Lincoln looked at the papers like they might reach out and handcuff him at any moment.

"It's been here all this time." Courtney leaned back in her desk chair, and it groaned. "Which is good because the fire department can't find their file."

Lincoln averted his eyes. His Adam's apple slid down and then up again.

"Lincoln," Hannah said softly. "Do you know why that file is missing at the fire department?"

Lincoln's gaze skittered toward her and then away again. He didn't speak for several seconds and then exhaled slowly. "As long as I'm confessing, I might as well get it all out. When I volunteered at the fire department in high school, I made sure to help out with some filing so I could have access to the files."

"But why?" Hannah finally asked. "Was there something in there you were worried about? Something more than what's in the insurance report? Because I can't see anything in here that implicates you."

Lincoln shook his head. "It just seemed like as long as that file existed, there was a chance it would get brought up again. Edward always planned to go into politics, and that can lead to people searching for skeletons in closets. I didn't want this skeleton coming out."

"But it was never *just* the fireworks, Lincoln." Lacy patted the report. "There was the gas burner too."

Hannah looked at the report once more. Why had she falsely remembered that the report said "oven" when the text clearly read "gas burner"?

Lincoln rubbed at the base of his skull, the same place where Hannah's stress headaches started. "Yeah, I know. But the file being destroyed made me feel safer."

"I can't believe you covered up something like this for all these years," Courtney said.

"I was young," Lincoln said quietly. "And at the time, it seemed to me that admitting a mistake like that would cost me everything."

Courtney narrowed her eyes. "And it didn't matter that it had already cost the Drakos family everything?"

Lincoln flinched and looked away. "If I could've told the truth and doing so would have erased what happened, then I would've chosen that. But I couldn't do anything for Theo or his mom at that point. What was done was done."

Courtney crossed her arms over her chest. "And you've always done what's best for Lincoln Lake."

Lincoln scowled. "We can't all be like you, Courtney. We can't all be perfect as pie."

"Pie." The word sprang from Hannah's mouth. She looked at Lacy. "Apple pie."

Lacy's eyebrows arched. "I get it. I think about food a lot these days, and that sounds amazing, but we'll have to take care of that craving later."

"No, *that's* why I assumed it was the oven that was left on, not a burner. Ivy Drakos made an apple pie for the Fourth of July party. She wouldn't have left a burner on. There wouldn't have been a need for a burner."

Courtney wasn't paying any attention to Hannah and Lacy's side conversation. "It's not about being *perfect*. It's about being *honest*." Courtney pressed her hand onto the stack of files in the corner of her desk. "You know what comes up time and time again in the complaints from our tenants? Broken promises. Dishonesty. It's at the root of this company."

"It's a good thing you're here to save us all." Lincoln crossed his arms over his chest. "You can take that up with your dad. Those were his decisions, not mine."

"And you did nothing to stop him. I guess now I understand why." Courtney leaned forward and fixed Lincoln with an unyielding stare. "Because he was keeping a secret for you, so of course you wouldn't do or say anything to upset him."

Hannah cleared her throat, drawing their attention to her. "Ivy Drakos made an apple pie for the Fourth of July party."

Courtney frowned. "Okay, and...?"

"She would've baked the pie in the *oven*." Lacy held up the report and tapped on the troublesome word *burner*. "There was no reason for the burner to be on."

"Maybe the burner wasn't on to make a pie," Courtney said, though it didn't sound like she believed it. "Maybe it was for dinner."

Hannah considered this a moment and then recalled the first time she spoke with Theo about the fire. "I don't think so. The firemen grilled hot dogs for everyone, and his mom was excited not to have to cook."

"That's right," Lincoln murmured. "I'd forgotten they used to do that. Those were the best hot dogs."

"And Theo said the whole place smelled like apple pie when they left the house that evening, and that he's never liked the smell since. But the house wouldn't have smelled like apple pie if a gas burner had been left on for any length of time."

Hannah was relieved to find that both Lincoln and Courtney appeared more pensive than angry.

Finally, Lincoln asked, "What exactly are you driving at, Hannah? Are you saying the fire was entirely my fault?"

"No, I'm not saying that. I think the burner *was* left on, but what if it wasn't Ivy or Theo who did that?"

A long furrow ran across Lincoln's brow. "Who else would it have been?"

Hannah hesitated and drew in a breath slowly through her nose. She had to be careful how she phrased this, because she wasn't pointing her finger at some random person.

But Courtney had already arrived there. "The lighter," she said in a hushed voice.

"What lighter?" Lincoln asked.

Hannah didn't feel like she should be the one to answer. She waited for Courtney to speak, but Courtney wasn't looking at any of them. Her eyes were unfocused and her jaw set.

"Lincoln..." Courtney's voice trailed off. She tapped her fingernails against her desk, clearly thinking something through.

"Yes?" Lincoln said after a moment.

Courtney didn't respond right away.

Lincoln glanced at Hannah, then Lacy, then back to Courtney. "What, Courtney?"

Courtney's lips pursed and then she nodded once, resolutely, before fixing her gaze on Lincoln. "This is going to seem like an odd question, but why did you go to Lake Blackberry that night?"

"On the Fourth of July?"

"It was way out in the country in the eighties. Why drive all the way out there just to shoot off those fireworks?"

Lincoln blinked at her a few times. His hair was disheveled and flopped onto his forehead, making it even easier for Hannah to imagine the scared teenager who lived inside him.

"Lincoln," Courtney pressed when he didn't seem inclined to answer. "Why?"

He inhaled slowly, then exhaled through his nose. "When Edward and I were helping unload fireworks, your dad mentioned he used to shoot them off out at Lake Blackberry."

Courtney leaned forward on her desk. "What *exactly* did Dad say?"

"That was pretty much it." Lincoln tucked his hands in the pockets of his slacks. "That he used to shoot off fireworks out there on a vacant lot. And that the lot was still there, right next to the house he owned."

Courtney nodded again, like this confirmed something she'd suspected. "Can you think of any reason why Dad would've *wanted* that fire started? Would've wanted that house burned down?"

Lincoln's eyes widened. "No. Maybe if the house was unoccupied and he was having trouble renting it out, then I could understand. But he would've been collecting rent from Ivy Drakos, so I can't see how losing the house would've benefited him at all."

Courtney tapped the closed file. "And yet, I'm pretty sure that's what happened."

Lincoln gave her a long, skeptical look. "I really don't think so."

"I can think of one way to find out." Courtney steepled her fingers and rested her chin on top of them. "I'll ask him."

Chapter Twenty-Two

Hannah and Lacy found Aunt Fiona, Theo, and Ivy still at the pizza place. A box containing their leftovers sat on the edge of the table, and all their glasses now held mostly ice. Apparently, the server had decided he was done with their group.

"Hannah," Aunt Fiona said with warm surprise as the two women approached. "And Lacy, hello. You've met Theo, I believe. This is his mother, Ivy Drakos. Ivy, this is Hannah's best friend, Lacy."

"Nice to meet you," Lacy said with a nod.

"Did you come back for your share of the pizza?" Theo asked with a teasing grin. "You took off so fast."

Hannah *was* hungry, but there'd be time for that later. "I'm sorry. A friend of mine called because she—well, she found something that she knew I'd be interested in."

Aunt Fiona sat up straighter with a hopeful smile on her face. "Something that will help you open the Hot Spot tonight?"

"No, it's unrelated."

"Maybe," Lacy cut in. She turned to Hannah. "I was actually thinking that this might be the piece of the Edward Lake puzzle that we were missing."

"Oh." Hannah's mind whirred with that idea. "That's an interesting thought."

"One to get to later." Lacy gestured to the three sitting at the table, who watched the two women with slightly puzzled expressions.

"Yes, you're right." Hannah brushed aside Lacy's suggestion. "As you know, Aunt Fiona and Theo, I've been looking into the fire a little bit—"

"Our fire?" Ivy asked, her tone high with surprise.

"Yes," Hannah said, then scanned their surroundings. The restaurant had emptied out, but it was good to be careful. After all, they hadn't confirmed anything, and she didn't want to spread unfounded rumors on the town grapevine. She gestured for Lacy to take the seat beside Aunt Fiona and grabbed a chair from another table for herself.

As succinctly as she could, Hannah quietly recounted everything that had transpired during the last couple of weeks, beginning with how she'd found Theo's treasures hidden behind a brick in her apartment, and how one bit of information had led to another except for the occasional odd gap, like the missing records from the fire department. She explained who Courtney Underhill was and the conversation she'd had with her, which led to Courtney's volunteering to check their company files to see if they had kept one on the fire.

"The one o'clock meeting that I was supposed to have today was with Courtney, and we were going to go through files together. But apparently, she got there early and found the file easily." Even though no one was nearby, Hannah still dropped her voice low. "She thinks the evidence suggests that Lawrence was involved in the fire."

Ivy leaned back in the booth and gaped at Hannah. "No, she must be wrong. He owned the house, so that makes no sense. What would he have gained from that?"

"That's still a bit unclear," Lacy said. "But we know he collected insurance money."

"Sure, but then he had no house to rent out," Theo said. "You have to remember that when Mom and I lived there, Lake Blackberry wasn't the desirable area it is now."

Hannah noted the time on the restaurant clock. "We have to hurry this conversation along because Courtney is about to confront her dad—"

"What?" Ivy's dark eyes went round. "This is madness."

"Courtney called her dad and asked him to meet her at the office to go over something that she found. She's going to ask him about the fire, and she wants you to be there to hear his answers. If you would like to be there, of course. It's your choice."

Ivy and Theo both looked too stunned to speak.

"But wouldn't their presence prevent Lawrence from telling the truth?" Aunt Fiona suggested. "If he *is* involved, they'd be the last people he'd want to know."

Hannah nodded. "That's why Courtney has suggested that we sit in their conference room where he can't see us. They have a phone system that allows Courtney to connect her office phone with the one they use for group calls. We'll be able to hear what they say, but they won't be able to hear us."

"But if we're going to do that, we need to leave soon." Lacy gave a nervous glance at her watch. "Like in the next minute or two."

"I don't know." Ivy toyed absently with the collar of her shirt. "I'm not sure it's a good idea."

"What if we discuss it in the car on our way?" Aunt Fiona asked. "Then if you decide you do want to hear what Lawrence has to say, there will still be time to get inside."

"That's a good idea," Theo said.

Hannah sent her aunt an appreciative smile. "The discussion between Courtney and her dad is going to happen whether we're there or not. The choice now is whether you want to be there to listen."

Theo gave a resolute nod. "I think we should, Mom. At the very least, I think we should take Fiona's suggestion and start heading that way."

Ivy bit her lower lip for a moment before giving a slight nod. "Okay. We can get in the car."

Getting everyone in the car took longer than Hannah would've liked, since neither Lacy nor Ivy were able to walk very fast. Then there was a short debate about who should sit up front, Ivy or Lacy. Lacy finally settled it by plopping herself in the back seat—as much as she *could* plop these days—beside Aunt Fiona, who'd taken the middle seat next to Theo.

"I don't feel good about taking the front seat when there's a pregnant woman in the car," Ivy protested, peering into the back with concern.

"The drive is five minutes long," Hannah said as she slid into the driver's seat. "And Lacy's a farmer. She's tough."

"It's true," Lacy confirmed.

On the brief drive back to the Lawrence Underhill Properties office, Hannah and Lacy took turns explaining what happened at the meeting they had with Courtney, as well as Lincoln's confession about his part in the fire.

"Oh, those Lake brothers." Ivy shook her head. "Full of mischief, but also somehow likable. Most of the time, anyway."

"I have some strong feelings of *dislike* for Edward Lake right now," Lacy grumbled from the back seat.

"Me too," Aunt Fiona said. "He's making Hannah's life very difficult."

"No time to go into that right now," Hannah said as she pulled the Subaru into a small parking lot down the street from Lawrence Underhill Properties at Courtney's request, so the car wouldn't be seen out front.

"What if this is a bad idea?" Ivy asked Theo as he helped her out of the passenger seat.

"One of the reasons you wanted to come back and see Blackberry Valley was because you wanted to heal from what happened here. This seems like a wonderful chance to get to the truth." Theo looked to Hannah and Lacy. "Because what these ladies are saying is right. You wouldn't have had a burner on that afternoon, Mom. The only thing you made was a pie."

"That's how I remember it, but it was a while ago." Ivy wrung her hands. "Maybe I boiled water for iced tea, and I left the burner on."

"I don't think you made tea, and we would've noticed a smell if the burner was left on." Theo placed his hands on his mother's shoulders and smiled lovingly at her. "This is a good opportunity that Hannah and Lacy have created for us. Let's use it well."

"And I don't mean to seem ungrateful, but…" The fear on Ivy's face broke Hannah's heart. "What if we go through all this and it's still clear that I'm the one to blame?"

"If that happens, I don't see how we'll be any worse off than we are right now," Theo said in a gentle voice. "For forty years, you've held yourself responsible."

Theo's voice was so calm and kind that Hannah was reminded of Liam. Of the way he spoke to her when she felt stressed or panicked, somehow making her feel like everything was going to work out fine. She missed him so much.

As she and Lacy led the group to the back door that Courtney instructed them to use, Hannah peeked at her phone. She'd sent Liam a text late that morning, right before leaving her apartment to pick up Aunt Fiona and take her out to the cemetery. His response had been brief, which Hannah knew to not take personally. Some of his work hours in Wyoming were like that—so busy that he barely had time to look at his phone, much less send a lengthy reply.

And Hannah certainly understood, because all she had time to type was MISSING YOU before they arrived at the door and she put her phone away. Lacy knocked, and a moment later Courtney opened the back door.

Courtney smiled at them all, though it was strained by the stress of the afternoon. "I was beginning to wonder. They'll be here soon, so come on in."

Lincoln stood down the hall, avoiding eye contact with all of them.

But Theo walked right to him with an outstretched hand. "Lincoln, it was an accident."

Lincoln looked up, his eyes searching Theo's face. "Thanks, Theo," he said in a gruff voice. His gaze shifted to Ivy and then dropped again. "I'm sorry for my part in what happened, Mrs. Drakos."

"We don't know anything for sure yet." Ivy's tone was as gentle as if Lincoln were her own child. "And you were just a boy."

Lincoln's eyes brimmed with tears, and Hannah felt her own eyes filling.

"Dad and Edward are going to be here in a few minutes," Courtney said. "Let's get you all to the conference room. We've set up everything so you'll be able to hear the four of us in my office, but we won't be able to hear you."

"Bless you for doing this," Ivy said to Courtney. "But I hope you know that it really might have been my fault the house burned down."

Courtney's smile was tinged with sadness. "Hopefully we're going to find out the truth today. I think it's about time, don't you?"

Ivy looked unsure, but they all followed Courtney to a back conference room, which consisted of a round table and chairs, a large window with the shades drawn, and a variety of potted plants. In the middle of the table was an elaborate phone with a large speaker, meant for group calls.

"I'm going to leave the lights off and the door closed so that Dad doesn't know anyone is back here," Courtney said as they all settled into seats. "Lincoln, will you make sure everything is set up correctly?"

Lincoln disappeared down the hallway, and a moment later they heard his voice—quiet but clear—over the speaker. "Testing, testing. Also, Courtney, I think I just heard a car outside."

"I better get out there." Courtney left, pulling the door shut behind her.

After a beat of silence, Aunt Fiona whispered, "This feels like a very macabre surprise party."

Hannah clenched her teeth to keep from giggling.

"I really hope I don't go into labor right now," Lacy added, shifting in the chair.

This time, Hannah couldn't fully keep her laugh trapped inside.

"When are you due?" Ivy whispered.

But then all their attention swung to the speaker in the middle of the table as Courtney said, "Hi, Dad. Hi, Edward."

"What's going on?" Edward asked, voice clipped. "You were very vague on the phone."

Hannah gripped the arms of her chair so she wouldn't leap out of the room, run down the hall, and demand an audience with Edward to discuss the fate of the Hot Spot. There were more important conversations that needed to be prioritized right now. Ivy and Theo had waited forty years for answers. She could wait too.

"What could be so critical that I had to drop everything and rush over here?" Lawrence demanded.

"Why don't we all take a seat?" Courtney responded.

Through the speaker came sounds of chairs scraping along the floor. Hannah's gaze traveled around the table. Aunt Fiona sat immediately to her left, and her hand gripped Theo's beneath the table. Theo sat beside his mother, his other hand resting on her shoulder. Ivy stared at the speaker while toying with a button on her blouse. On the other side of Hannah, Lacy shifted in her seat, clearly struggling to get comfortable.

"Dad, I've come across something in our files that I'd like to talk to you about. This is regarding the fire that happened on our property, the one that destroyed the rental house that was there before ours."

Silence. Then a huff of a laugh. "You had me rush over here to talk about a fire that happened decades ago?"

"Yes. I've been looking through the file, and I'm confused about—"

"What file are you talking about?" Lawrence interrupted.

"The file we had here." Another silence. "Did you not know we had a file here?"

"Who put that together?"

"Considering it was 1986, I assume Minnie created the file."

"Did either of you know there was a file here?" Lawrence asked.

Hannah assumed his question was directed at the Lake brothers.

"You seem concerned about there being a file, Dad." Courtney's words weren't sharp, but they were certainly pointed. "Why shouldn't there be one? After all, there was an insurance claim involved, which means paperwork. Wouldn't Minnie have been expected to create a file for an incident of that nature?"

No one answered immediately.

Finally, Lawrence asked, "Is that the file?"

"It is. The reason Lincoln and I called you both in here is—"

"Give it to me."

"You can see the file in a minute, Dad. We called you both in here because—"

"Not 'in a minute.' I'm your father. Give me the file *now*."

At the sound of Lawrence yelling, Hannah leaned back from the speaker.

There was a squeak of a chair, like the one Courtney's made when she leaned backward or forward. "You're obviously very worried about what this file contains, and I'm not surprised. After looking through the report carefully, I no longer think that fire was an accident." After a beat, Courtney asked, "Why are you looking at Edward and Lincoln?"

Even through the speaker, the silence was heavy.

"Look, boys," Lawrence said, which was funny when Hannah considered that Edward and Lincoln were close in age to Aunt Fiona and Theo. Apparently to Lawrence, they were still *boys.* "I've protected you as long as I can. It's time to come clean. Courtney, the truth is that Edward and Lincoln started that fire—accidentally, of course—because they were messing around with fireworks on the vacant lot next door."

Everyone in the conference room leaned closer to the speaker, awaiting the next words.

"Edward," Courtney said in the same firm but calm voice she'd been using the entire conversation. "Is there anything you'd like to add?"

"There isn't much else to say." Edward sounded resigned. Defeated. "We weren't trying to do anything more than have a little fun on the Fourth of July. We certainly never meant to start that fire."

In the following silence, Hannah glanced across the table at Theo and Ivy, who were both staring at the speaker with such intensity, Hannah wouldn't have been surprised if *that* caught fire next.

"Are you sure it was you who started the fire?" Courtney asked quietly. "Because Lincoln said you guys never saw the fire. That you didn't even know it had happened until you got back to the party."

"That's true. If we'd known, we'd have tried to put it out, of course. Theo was a friend of ours. We felt awful about what happened."

"Courtney," Lawrence said, "I know you can be dogged about pursuing the truth. You've always been that way. But they were only boys, and they can't undo what happened. I don't see any benefit to this being shared outside of these four walls."

"Wait," Edward said, sounding as though he'd just had a realization. "Courtney, have you already spoken to someone else about this? Because I know the fire department has been looking for their records of the fire."

"Have they?" Courtney asked.

"Yes. I overheard the owner of the Hot Spot talking about it with one of the firemen. But I don't think she'll be a problem. I've taken some measures to preoccupy her."

Hannah froze. She could feel the eyes of everyone in the room shift to her. So that was why Edward hadn't been calling her back. *He* was responsible. *He wanted* the Hot Spot to stay closed.

Hannah looked at her best friend. "You were right."

Lacy grimaced. "I wish I felt more like gloating."

"'Measures to preoccupy her'?" Courtney repeated. "What does that mean?"

"I don't owe you an explanation, Courtney."

"Are *you* the reason Hannah had to close the Hot Spot to install that grease trap?"

Lacy's fists clenched. "Oh, just wait until I get out of here."

The sight of her pregnant friend balling her fists was enough to make Hannah's own anger dissipate. She giggled and patted Lacy's hand. "I have a feeling this problem is about to go away."

"That's despicable," Courtney continued. "Did you know about this, Lincoln?"

"No," Lincoln said.

But the word was barely out of Lincoln's mouth before Courtney carried on with her rant. "I can't believe you would really attempt to drive that poor woman out of business. This is like your ex-wife all over again."

"I'm not trying to drive her out of business," Edward said, voice stiff and indignant. "I have no intention of *actually* making her install a grease trap. I'll make the whole thing disappear in the next day or two."

"Do you care at all about how much money you're costing her or her employees? Or are you really so selfish that you don't care, so long as nobody finds out about a mistake you made when you were a teenager?"

"Not just a mistake," Lawrence pointed out. "They could've done jail time."

"It doesn't matter," Lincoln said, his voice soft. Defeated. "I'm tired of carrying the weight of what happened. Aren't you, Edward?"

Edward guffawed. "What are you saying? We turn ourselves in *now*? Forty years later? Don't you think our wives and kids would have something to say about that?"

"None of this is necessary," Lawrence said, speaking louder than before. "The house belonged to me, and I've known all along that you were responsible for that fire. In my view, we're square, and that's what matters. Courtney, are you satisfied now?"

"No," Courtney said, her voice gentle. Sad. "Because I don't believe Edward and Lincoln *are* responsible for the fire." There was a rustling of papers and then Courtney asked, "Dad, why is your lighter in these pictures?"

Hannah held her breath.

"Is it?" Lawrence finally said. "I don't think so. You can barely see it with the quality of the picture and how small that object is. Whatever it is."

"Here's a magnifying glass."

There were shuffling noises, but no one spoke for a while.

"Well, I guess that answers the question of what happened to my favorite lighter." Lawrence's laugh sounded forced, but Hannah reminded herself it was also distorted by the speaker.

Courtney's voice was unyielding as she said, "I'm surprised that whoever investigated the fire didn't ask you about it."

"There were other lighters in the house too," Lawrence said. "Probably in a kitchen drawer."

"But why was *yours* there?" Courtney pressed. "Maybe whoever inspected the fire assumed it was Ivy's or Theo's, but *I* know better, Dad."

After a beat of silence, Lawrence said, "I'd been there earlier in the week to fix a leaky sink. I probably left it then."

"That's not true," Ivy whispered.

"Why would you have been fixing something yourself instead of calling someone?" Courtney asked.

"I can't recall why I did that day. My maintenance guy must have been sick or something. It was a long time ago, Courtney."

"Like he would have ever sent anybody," Ivy grumbled to Theo. "How many times did I complain about our hot water, and did that ever get fixed? No."

Theo patted his mom's shoulder, both to comfort and to hush her, Hannah suspected.

"Let me get this straight. You think your dad is responsible for the fire?" Edward's question rolled out slowly, as though he was also pondering the idea.

"Of course she doesn't," Lawrence said. "That's ridiculous. Why would I burn down a house I owned?"

"I'm still not sure," Courtney said in that calm, even tone. "But I think now is the ideal time for you to come clean and explain it to me. Edward and Lincoln, can either of you think of a single time Dad ever went and fixed something himself at one of the properties? Even if maintenance couldn't get to the issue in a reasonable amount of time?"

Nobody spoke.

"Me neither," Courtney continued. "My best theory is that you did it for the insurance money. That's why it had to look like the resident had left the burner on, and why you had to come up with some plausible reason why the fire would've started. So, you asked Edward and Lincoln to help you unload the fireworks, then, because you knew the type of boys they were, you suggested an ideal spot for shooting off a few before leaving them alone when they could easily pocket some of the supply."

Edward's voice was barely audible on the speaker. "He *is* the one who suggested we go out there."

"Courtney, how can you think a thing like this after all I've done for you?" Lawrence's words vibrated with anger. "After all I've built for you?"

"I'm not denying that you built a successful company," Courtney said quietly. "I'm asking who really paid the price for your success."

"I never should've left this company to you. This is how you treat me after all I've done for you? After all I've done for *all* of you?

Especially you two boys. Didn't I keep you out of trouble when you were nothing more than a couple of scared teenagers?"

"You *put* us in trouble," Lincoln snapped. "You made us think we were responsible for what happened at Theo's house, but Courtney's right. The only reason your lighter would have been there was because *you* were there. And I think you used it to set off a fire of your own so Edward and I would think all this time that we were responsible. So that we would feel like we *owed* you."

"Like it's been so terrible for you," Lawrence growled.

Hannah sucked in a breath. Lawrence wasn't denying the accusations anymore. He was rationalizing. She cut a look to Lacy, who had noticed as well.

"I gave you both good jobs. I helped you get elected, Edward. And I built this company and handed it to you, Courtney, when I could've sold it. Is it so much to ask for you not to look down your noses at me because it wasn't built according to your overly strict moral code?"

"I just want to know why," Courtney said, a touch of pleading entering her voice. "As far as I can tell, this is the only rental property you ever burned to the ground. Why'd you do it? Were you angry with the Drakoses?"

"It had nothing to do with them."

"Then why?"

"Location, location, location." Lincoln was the one who murmured the well-known mantra of the real estate business. "Why didn't I see it before? You knew what was about to happen at Lake Blackberry. Didn't you, Lawrence?"

Hannah and the others in the conference room leaned closer to the speaker. The silence stretched agonizingly long.

"I had a fishing buddy on the council," Lawrence said in a resigned voice. "He made a comment about the plans to develop the lake into a park. I knew immediately that property values were going to skyrocket. But the company was already stretched thin financially, and I had a limited window to get the cash together to buy up other property around the lake. I had to get it done *before* the announcement was made."

"So you collected the insurance money, then used it to buy property around the lake?" Courtney's tone clearly expressed her outrage.

"Don't you think I've had my regrets over the years?" Lawrence snapped. "You could never understand, Courtney, because everything has always been handed to you. But not me. I started with nothing and had to work hard for everything our family has. Big opportunities only come around so often, and I knew I had to take my shot. Regardless."

"You mean regardless of who it hurt along the way." Courtney's disgust was clear, even through the speaker. "Regardless of whether you had to destroy somebody's *home* and all their possessions."

"I made sure they were out of the house. And that they had some money to get started in their new life." Now Lawrence sounded as though he was withholding tears. "Don't look at me like that, honey."

"How else am I supposed to look at you? You know Ivy and Theo Drakos deserve an explanation, an apology and, frankly, much more."

"If I could, I would," Lawrence said. "I promise you that."

"Well, good news, Dad. They're here now." Courtney's voice boomed through the speaker. "Can everyone please come in here?"

Chapter Twenty-Three

Hannah just sat there, grappling with Courtney's request, which made her feel like she was on a daytime talk show episode. But Ivy jumped to her feet. The elderly woman was already out the conference room door, Theo and Aunt Fiona close behind her, while Lacy was still pushing herself up from the chair with a grunt.

"I envy how fast she moves," Lacy huffed as she and Hannah followed.

"You know who I *don't* envy right now?" Hannah murmured. "Lawrence."

As spacious as Courtney's office was, it had quickly become crowded now that the Lake brothers, Lawrence, Ivy, and Theo were inside. Aunt Fiona hovered in the doorway, and Hannah and Lacy stood beside her.

Hannah's eyes immediately found Edward's. He turned away, and his face grew bright red.

Ivy stood at her full height—which couldn't have been more than five foot two—and glared at Lawrence. "Well, Mr. Underhill, I'm ready for that apology."

Lawrence looked up at her, his eyes wide and his mouth agape. His gaze traveled to Theo, then the three women in the doorway, before landing back on Ivy.

"Well, Dad?" Courtney prompted. "I think you have something to say to Mrs. Drakos."

Lawrence glanced at his daughter and then down at his feet. "Mrs. Drakos, I…I'm sorry."

"Do you have any idea what it's like to think you're responsible for the most traumatic thing that ever happened to your child?" Ivy's voice was quiet but commanding.

Lawrence continued to stare at his lap. To Hannah's surprise, a tear fell and darkened a spot on his pant leg. Then another. "I'm sorry." His voice cracked on the word *sorry*, and he covered his face with his hands. "I'm so sorry."

"I've spent forty years thinking that my mistake cost my son a life he loved. That's not something that an apology can fix, however heartfelt it may be."

"You're right. I can't undo the choice I made and what it cost your family." Lawrence swallowed and glanced at Ivy, then at Theo. "I can offer you my apology, and I can offer you a payment for damages, but that's all I have."

Ivy peered down at him, considering. "The last time we spoke, I took money from you because I was afraid of involving anybody official. I won't make that mistake again this time. I'm going to speak to a lawyer and see what my options are."

Courtney wore an expression of grim resignation. "I think that's what I would do in your situation, Mrs. Drakos."

Ivy held Courtney's gaze before looking back to Lawrence. "If I *don't* pursue legal action, Mr. Underhill, I want you to know that it's because of the character and integrity of your daughter. I've been told by these women"—Ivy pointed to Hannah and Lacy—"that

Courtney has gone to great efforts to improve the lives of your company's tenants. The only reason I'm considering not taking action is because of the changes Courtney is making to how business is done here. I don't want to do anything that would punish *her*."

More tears landed on Lawrence's lap. "She's always been a good girl. She turned out better than I deserved."

"God is gracious like that," Ivy said.

"Yes, He is," Courtney put in. She looked at Theo. "Is there anything you'd like to say, Theo? This was a crime against you as well."

"No, ma'am." Theo put a hand on Ivy's shoulder. "I trust my mom to handle this in the way she sees fit."

Ivy smiled up at her son, her eyes shining. Hannah could see how much his words meant to her.

Lacy cleared her throat. "I don't think we're quite done with apologies in here yet. Edward, it seems to me that you have something to say to Hannah too."

Courtney leaned back in her chair and swiveled to face Edward, who had been standing quietly in the corner, as if he hoped he might be mistaken for a potted plant. "Yes, I think he does."

Hannah fixed her gaze on Edward, though it seemed he was having trouble doing the same. He looked everywhere in the room but at her.

"I'm sorry for the trouble, Hannah." The words were gruff. "I was trying to protect my little brother."

Aunt Fiona gave a dismissive snort of laughter. "And maybe your own hide too?"

Edward ducked his head. "I'm very sorry."

Hannah inhaled deeply and thought about Ivy's words moments ago—*God is gracious*. He'd certainly been gracious to her over the years as she'd bumbled through life, and with His help, she could also be gracious to Edward.

"If the Hot Spot is going to open at its usual time, then I need to get going," Hannah said. "I assume the city won't have a problem with us reopening?"

Edward swallowed hard. "Of course not."

"Good." Hannah nodded. "Then I accept your apology. And I hope you—I hope *all* of you—will come for dinner tonight."

The Hot Spot kitchen was pure chaos as Jacob and Hannah worked to serve their guests, but Hannah couldn't remember the last time she'd smiled so hard or enjoyed her work so much. None of their usual prep work had happened that afternoon, which meant that every order that came in was more complex to prepare than usual. Even so, there was nowhere else Hannah would rather be.

Except maybe with Liam.

She glanced at her phone. After everything that had happened at Lawrence Underhill Properties, Hannah had sent him a rushed text that said, CAN'T GO INTO DETAILS NOW, BUT THE HOT SPOT WILL BE OPEN TONIGHT!

CAN'T WAIT TO HEAR WHAT HAPPENED, he'd replied an hour later. MAYBE YOU'LL GET A BREAK DURING WORK, AND WE CAN TALK?

But Hannah wasn't so sure she would. She had managed to text back the thumbs-up emoji, but the Hot Spot demanded 100 percent of her focus this evening.

"I spent some time thinking about the fall menus today," Jacob said as he pulled chicken out of the fryer. He hadn't stopped smiling since his arrival that evening. "Maybe we'll have time to go over them early next week. I already know there are a few items on my list that you'll say aren't a good fit, because I made a whole list of dinners inspired by Julia Child. But I'm hoping you'll hear me out."

Hannah imagined the Julia Child-inspired dishes, alongside the menu of loaded baked potatoes Jacob had suggested last weekend, and had to repress a laugh. "I'm looking forward to it," she said. And she meant it. "You're right that it's about time to be thinking about fall menus. Which is crazy."

"I know. Can't believe fall will be knocking on our door before we know it."

The next few months would bring more than a mere seasonal menu change. There was about to be a new person in the world, a person Hannah already loved deeply. And in November, she would cease to be Hannah Prentiss and would become Hannah Berthold. She would be living somewhere new and figuring out what it meant to be Liam's wife rather than simply Hannah.

Yes, a lot of change awaited her on the horizon, but the idea didn't feel quite as scary as it once had. Not with God's unfailing love and guidance.

"Hannah?" Dylan called from the doorway. "We need you in the dining room."

Hannah whirled to face him. "What?"

"We need you in the dining room," Dylan repeated. "There's a situation at Table Eight. Leave your chef's coat in here."

She turned back to the food she'd been chopping. She *really* didn't have time for this. "What's going on? Why should I leave my...?"

But Dylan had already gone, and Hannah was left staring at the door swinging shut behind him.

Hannah gave Jacob an exasperated look, but he just grinned and shrugged, like they weren't completely swamped. "Go. I'm fine for a bit."

Grumbling, Hannah unbuttoned the coat and hung it on its hook. A "situation" at a table didn't sound like a good thing. She wished Dylan had stuck around long enough to tell her what to expect so she could mentally prepare for how to respond to what was probably a ruffled guest.

She peeked around for Dylan as she exited the kitchen but spotted only Raquel. "Hey, do you know what the situation is at Table Eight?" she asked her waitress.

Raquel only shrugged as she breezed past Hannah. Which was unusually dismissive behavior from her. Hannah felt the sting of it—until she rounded the corner and saw for herself what the "situation" was.

She gasped with delight at the sight of a candlelit table for two, from which Liam Berthold grinned at her. "Liam!"

Hannah sprinted through the dining room. Liam stood, his arms open wide. Hannah jumped into them and flung her arms around his neck, causing the restaurant guests to burst into applause. Ordinarily, Hannah would've been embarrassed to be the center of attention like this, but she was so overcome with joy at the sight of him that she didn't even care that everyone was staring.

"Good surprise?" he asked, his words warm in her ear.

Hannah's eyes brimmed with happy tears as she beamed up at him. "The *best* surprise."

He squeezed her hands. "Will you have dinner with me? I thought about ordering for both of us, but Dylan said he wasn't sure if you'd be able to pause right now with how crazy your day has been."

"There's nothing I'd love more than to eat with you. We're through the worst of the rush, and Jacob said he was fine back there." Hannah took the seat across from Liam but continued holding his hands. She drank in the sight of him. He was freshly shaven and wearing a brown shirt that she'd bought for him because it matched his eyes. "I can't believe you're here."

Dylan materialized at the table, mouth tipped in a mischievous smile. "Good evening," he said with mock formality. "Are you ready to order, or do you need a few more minutes to look over the menu?"

Hannah grinned up at him. "Thank you for telling me to leave my chef's coat in the kitchen."

He broke character and smiled back at her. "Of course."

"I'd like the Five Alarm Burger." Liam winked at Hannah, "Aside from you, that's what I've thought about the most since I've been gone."

"I'll have the same," Hannah said. "And tell Jacob to put extra flourish on mine."

Dylan laughed. "You got it."

When Dylan walked away, Liam squeezed Hannah's hands. "I thought I was coming home to swoop in and rescue you from the evils of new city codes. What happened today?"

Hannah took a deep breath and walked him through the events of the day, from the meeting with Courtney to uncovering the truth about the fire that night. She'd just finished her monologue when Dylan approached with their burgers.

When he set Hannah's plate in front of her, she burst out laughing. Jacob had clearly enjoyed himself. He'd included multiple frilly toothpicks, and there was a decadent swirl of raspberry chipotle sauce across her plate.

"This is perfect," Hannah said. "My compliments to the chef."

"I'll pass that along," Dylan said with a grin. "I'll leave you two alone, but flag me down if you want something else."

Liam prayed over their dinner, and Hannah felt like her heart might burst out of her chest with all the happiness she felt. The restaurant was open. Liam was home. She was going to be his wife in a few short months. Life was so, so good.

After saying "amen," Liam released her hands and took an oversize bite of his Five Alarm Burger.

"As good as you remember?" Hannah asked.

He nodded enthusiastically. As soon as he swallowed, he added, "Even better."

"That's what I like to hear."

"Back to what you were saying," Liam went on. "Edward Lake is *not* getting my vote next time around. I can't believe he did that to you."

"He was scared." Hannah shrugged. "People do crazy things when they're scared."

"Even so." Liam opened his mouth to say something else, but his gaze fixed on someone behind Hannah, and his smile shifted to his polite variety.

Hannah turned to find Aunt Fiona approaching the table. "Sorry to interrupt," she said, looking sheepish.

Hannah leaped out of her seat to hug her. "This is perfect. I didn't realize you guys were still here. Aunt Fiona, this is my fiancé, Liam. Liam, my aunt Fiona."

"So nice to finally meet you," Liam said as they shook hands.

"I feel like I already know you." Aunt Fiona grinned at him. "I understand you've been up in Wyoming helping with the wildfires?"

"Yes, ma'am. Just rolled back into town today. I was trying to rescue Hannah, but she rescued herself before I could get back." He winked at Hannah. "No surprise there."

"She's quite the woman," Aunt Fiona said. "I've loved getting to spend time with her these last couple of weeks."

"How much longer are you in town?" Liam asked, popping a french fry into his mouth.

"I leave the day after tomorrow, unfortunately."

Disappointment settled in Hannah's chest. She loved having Aunt Fiona in town and wasn't ready for her to leave yet. "You do?"

"I know. I'm not ready to go either. But the good news is that in the future we'll have more opportunities to see each other." She grinned at Hannah. "I've just applied for a nursing job in Louisville."

Hannah gasped and again leaped up to throw her arms around Aunt Fiona. "That's the best news. You'll be so close."

"I know." Aunt Fiona squeezed her back. "I'm really excited about getting to see all of you more. And getting to know you better, Liam."

Beyond Aunt Fiona, Hannah could see Theo and Ivy at a table, chatting in the warm glow of the restaurant.

Hannah pulled back and grinned at Aunt Fiona. "I bet I know somebody else who's excited you're going to be moving to Louisville."

Aunt Fiona ducked her head, but it didn't hide how pink her cheeks had turned. "It's possible I factored him into my decision."

Hannah snorted a laugh. "Oh, it's *possible*? Is that all?"

Aunt Fiona shrugged and then urged Hannah back into her seat. "Tomorrow night, we're going to have a dinner at your dad and Gordon's. I've already talked to Drew and Allison, and they'll be there with the kids. Gordon also invited Ryder, as well as Maeve and her crew. Theo and his mom are sticking around town, so they'll be there too. Any chance the two of you can make it?"

"Absolutely," Liam said before Hannah could respond. "We'll be there."

"Great. I'll let you enjoy your time together now, but I look forward to seeing you both tomorrow. We'll probably get the Slip 'N Slide out, so dress accordingly."

Hannah laughed. "I can't wait."

"She seems great," Liam said as Aunt Fiona walked back to where Theo and his mom sat.

"She's the best."

Liam reached across the table and squeezed her hand. "Not the *best*. But great. I'm looking forward to tomorrow night."

"Me too." Hannah smiled at him, feeling peace settle into her soul. "Actually, I'm looking forward to a lot of things."

From the Author

Dear Reader,

Sometimes when I'm at a crowded event—like a concert or sporting event—and I'm limited in what I'm allowed to bring in, I will think, "If I had to run for my life and this was all I had with me, how far could I make it?" I suppose that's why one of my favorite parts of writing *Forged in Fire* was figuring out what Theo would've had in his pockets the night of the fire. I was a pretty dramatic teenager myself, and the idea of hiding my treasured possessions the way he did definitely would have appealed to me!

The opportunity to explore Blackberry Valley through teenage eyes was really fun, especially since young Fiona still had a lot to learn about who she was, like we all do when we're teens! The best part of stepping back in time with Fiona was the chance to experience the young adult version of Hannah's mother, Frieda. We've heard about her during this series, and I loved the chance to explore who she was and what the early days of her relationship with Gabriel Prentiss looked like.

Like Hannah in this story, I often feel a mix of both excitement and anxiety when I think about the months and years to come. Exploring the book's theme that God can be trusted even when I don't understand the path He's put me on was a great reminder as

I went through my own seasons of change during the writing of this book.

Hope you have a wonderful summer,
Stephanie Coleman

About the Author

Stephanie Coleman is the author of several contemporary young adult series, as well as two historical young adult novels. Since 2010, Stephanie has been encouraging the next generation of writers at her website, GoTeenWriters.com, which has been on the Writer's Digest Best Websites for Writers list since 2017. She lives in the Kansas City area, where she loves plotting big and small adventures to enjoy with her husband and three children.

The Hot Spotlight

Outdated Features of Older Homes

As a child, I dreamed of moving into an old house and discovering something amazing like a hidden room, a box of letters under a floorboard, or initials scratched into a doorpost. While some people who buy older homes do get lucky and find something cool—like an old letter and a compass belonging to the sweet boy who befriended your aunt in high school—you're more likely to find a quirky feature like one of these in an older home.

Phone niche or nooks: Because phones used to be so bulky, specific alcoves or cubbies were built into walls to house them. You're most likely to find these in houses from the 1920s or 1930s.

Button light switches: These were introduced in the late nineteenth century and remained popular until the midtwentieth century when the toggle switches we use now took over. While the buttons have an aesthetic charm and are making a comeback, they had a tendency to get stuck.

Boot scrapers: This is a cast iron structure low to the ground, commonly found at front doors. Their purpose is pretty obvious—scraping mud off your boots before going into the house. These were very common before paved sidewalks and roads became commonplace.

A razor slit in medicine cabinets: This feature was a small hole in the medicine cabinet where one could dispose of used razor blades. You might ask, “Where did the razor blades go?” and the answer is, “Into the wall.” Homeowners who remove drywall in these homes often find a pile of old razor blades awaiting them!

Picture-hanging molding: Picture rails or picture-hanging molding became common in the 1840s as a way to hang pictures from a movable hook without damaging the wall’s surface. By the 1940s, the method we use now for hanging pictures became standard, and builders stopped installing the extra molding.

While my childhood dream has come true and I do live in an older home, I haven’t found anything cool and quirky.

Yet.

From the Hot Spot Kitchen

HANNAH'S PINEAPPLE JICAMA SALSA

Ingredients:

1 fresh pineapple, diced small (approximately 2 cups)

1½ cups jicama (about half a large jicama), diced small

½ cup red onion, finely diced

1 jalapeno pepper, seeded and finely diced (if you like it spicy, leave the seeds in!)

1 red bell pepper, seeded and finely diced

2 tablespoons of lime juice (or the juice of one lime)

½ teaspoon salt

2 tablespoons fresh cilantro, chopped (optional)

Directions:

Combine all the ingredients in a bowl, then stir to mix. Let the salsa sit in the refrigerator for several hours before serving with tortilla chips.

Read on for a sneak peek of another exciting book in the *Mysteries of Blackberry Valley* series!

The Big Picture

BY LAURA BRADFORD

Stepping onto the flagstone walkway, Hannah Prentiss silently drank in the view of the modest two-story house flanked by a pair of dogwood trees. There, on that early August day, the branches played host to green leaves, but in her mind's eye she could imagine the countless white flowers they would produce come spring.

"Is that a good sigh or a bad sigh I just heard?"

She pulled her focus from the scene in her head and fixed it, instead, on the handsome, dark-haired man standing between her and Tasha Bemis, the Realtor who'd patiently taken them through nearly every house with a For Sale sign in their hometown of Blackberry Valley, Kentucky. "I didn't realize I sighed," she said, smiling up at her fiancé, Liam Berthold.

"You did. Though, based on that sparkle in your eyes, I think I have my answer."

Again, Hannah gazed at the house, resting her cheek on Liam's upper arm as she did. "It's really cute. And..." She paused as she took in the wide front porch, the flower boxes on the front windows, the soft yellow clapboard siding, and the feeling of peace that filled her from the inside out. "*Welcoming*, isn't it?"

He wrapped his arm around her shoulders and squeezed. "It's saying the same thing to me." He turned to Tasha. "Now, the MLS says this place is older than I am, and I know that's the case for everything in this general area of town, but it seems newer than that somehow."

"That's because the sellers made some major exterior improvements when they bought the place six months ago," Tasha said.

Hannah and Liam exchanged glances of concern before Hannah turned back to Tasha. "Did they uncover a problem with the house that made them want to sell so quickly?"

Opening the folder in her hands, Tasha ran her finger down the printout it contained. "No. They purchased it remotely while working overseas and commissioned contractors to spruce up its curb appeal, as you can see. Just as they were getting ready to return to the States and move in, the husband got a job offer in Seattle that was too good to pass up. So they put it back on the market."

"Are you saying they never lived here at all?" Hannah asked.

Tasha nodded. "Never lived in or even saw it in person."

"Wow." Hannah looked from the house, to Liam, and then back to Tasha. "And *before* they bought it?"

"It's been owned by just one other family, the Van Lutens."

"As in the Van Luten twins?" Liam asked.

"Their parents, Owen and Julie, but yes."

Hannah turned her thoughts from the rocking chairs she was picturing on the front porch and focused on the conversation. "Should I know this Van Luten family?"

Liam shrugged. "Maybe not. The twins—Scotty and Sal—were seniors when I started at the high school, so you'd have only been in seventh grade. *I* knew them because they were the stars of the football team that year. Everyone in school knew who they were." He turned back to Tasha. "I don't remember them returning after they went to college, but their parents were the only owners until six months ago?"

"They were. When the boys went off to school, Owen and Julie left to help Julie's ailing parents where they were living. Nebraska, maybe? Somewhere in that part of the country, anyway. From what I heard through the grapevine at the time, Julie died from an undetected heart issue within weeks of her parents. Owen was so broken up over Julie's death that he never came back to Blackberry Valley. When he finally passed away a year or so ago, this house was left to the boys. They wanted to sell it right away, but there was some squabble between them, and it ended up in probate."

Hannah took a moment to process the information as, once again, she took in the porch and the trees and the home's beckoning feel. "So, other than the exterior sprucing here in the front, this place has been without a family for quite some time."

"Close to twenty-three years by my calculation," Liam said, glancing back at Tasha for confirmation.

"Yes. Which means it's more than ready for a new family." Tasha closed the folder and tucked it under her arm. "Do you want to look inside? See what you think about the rest of it?"

"Absolutely," Hannah and Liam said in unison, then laughed as Tasha led them to the front porch.

At the base of the steps, Tasha stopped and gestured to the quiet street behind them. "This being a cul-de-sac makes this a peaceful neighborhood, since there's no traffic passing through. And later on, if you have children, it's a fairly short walk through the woods to Summit Street Park."

Hannah blinked with surprise. "You mean the public playground just past the high school?" she asked.

"One and the same." Tasha pressed a series of buttons on the lockbox mounted to the front door. When they heard an answering beep, she retrieved the key, unlocked the door, and motioned them inside. "Since this is an empty house, I'll wait out here. But, as with all the houses we've looked at so far today, take your time, snap some pictures, imagine how it might be with your furniture, your touches, et cetera."

"Thanks, Tasha." Hannah stepped into the front hallway, waited for Liam to close the door behind them, and then walked with him into a large room to their right. Together, they inspected an old chair rail that ran around the room with wainscoting below. "Oh wow, what a gorgeous dining room this would make, Liam. Can't you just picture our families eating here with us on Thanksgiving or Christmas?"

He smiled. "I can, actually." He crossed to the wall and ran his hand along the piece of molding. "But I'd want to replace this chair rail with a new one. Not because the nicks and scratches on it bother me all that much, but because I want any nicks and scratches to tell *our* stories, not someone else's."

Stepping in beside him, Hannah wrapped her arm around his back for a quick squeeze. "*Our stories*. I like that."

"So do I." He kissed the top of her head and then held his hand out for her to take. "Let's see what's next."

Slowly, they made their way from room to room, admiring the spacious kitchen with room for an island if they opted to add one, the cozy family room with a fireplace, built-in bookshelves, and big windows, and a small laundry room, which neither of them had in their respective apartments. As they approached the back of the house, they peeked into the home's main-floor powder room to the left of the switchback staircase before coming to a full stop just outside an open doorway to its right. The room it led to boasted a view of the wooded backyard through two vertical windows.

"An extra bedroom?" she asked.

Liam guided her into the room. "Unofficially, maybe. But officially, it can't be. There's no closet."

"We could put a desk in here and make it an office," she suggested.

"If that's what you want, that's what we'll do," he said. "As long as we're together, enjoying this place."

"*This* place?" she teased. "Have we decided this will be our home, Chief?"

Liam nodded. "If you think so too. I like what I've seen here better than any of the other houses we've looked at so far. It's cozy, yet spacious. The curb appeal is fantastic. It's got easy access to the firehouse for me, and to the restaurant for you. What do you think?"

"I like this place too. *A lot.*" She took a moment to breathe in the empty space, releasing it along with a smile. "If we didn't make this an office, it could be a library."

"Or a playroom," he added, grinning. "For those kids Gramps is already talking about us having."

They exited the room and made their way to the second floor for a tour of the home's three bedrooms and two full bathrooms. When they were done, Liam followed her back through every room in the house on both floors as she snapped pictures with her phone from various angles.

"I like this place, Hannah," Liam said. "I *really* like this place."

Slowly, she lowered her phone to her side and gave in to the happy squeal she couldn't hold back if she tried. "I do too, Liam. Very, very much."

He reached for her hand and then brushed his lips across the fingers she'd entwined with his. "Let's go join Tasha, take some pictures of the front, and then the back of the house and the yard. Sound good?"

"Sounds great. Let's do it."

Outside, Hannah took pictures of the porch, the window boxes, and the dogwood trees, and then one of Liam standing in front of it all with his arms outstretched and a mile-wide smile on his handsome face. When she had what she wanted to capture of the home's front, they wandered around to the back. There, while Liam walked the tree line and what appeared to be a well-worn path into the woods, Hannah took a few pictures, noted a tattered window screen lying on the patio that they'd need to repair at some point, and was just starting to call out to Liam when her phone vibrated in her hand.

A glance at the screen showed an incoming call from Lacy Minyard, her best friend. Holding her finger in the air, Hannah smiled at Tasha. "I'm sorry, but I need to take this. My friend is about to have a baby any day now, and I need to answer her calls."

"No problem at all," Tasha said, stepping away to join Liam.

Hannah held the phone to her ear. "Is it time?"

Lacy laughed. "Well, hello to you too. But in answer to your question, no. Baby Minyard is happy exactly where he or she is for the time being."

"That's disappointing."

"It's going to happen, Hannah."

"I know. I'm just excited to meet my godchild."

A second laugh from Lacy was interrupted by a yawn. "I am too. I'm also trying to resist another nap, which is why I'm calling you. So, what are you up to this fine Monday?"

"Liam and I are looking at houses today."

"Oh, right. You told me that at church yesterday. I'm sorry. I didn't mean to interrupt."

"No, it's okay. But can I check in with you later?"

"Of course."

"But if something suddenly changes in the next hour or so regarding the baby, you call right away, okay?"

Lacy yawned again. "Yes, Mom."

"Hey!"

"Just teasing. I know you love me."

"Forever and always." When Lacy ended the call, Hannah glanced back at the broken patio and the tattered screen, then called for Liam to join her. When he did, she pointed from the screen to the spot where it had clearly come from—a small window on the first floor between a larger window on one side and the two vertical ones on the other. "Remind me what room that window is to?" she asked.

Liam walked to the screen, picked it up, inspected it, and then set it back down on the patio. "The half bath?"

"No. It only had one window, and that's there," she said, pointing to the window on the exterior's far right. "And those vertical ones on the other side are the ones in that unofficial bedroom/study thing."

He grinned. "You mean playroom?"

"Yes, *Gramps*, I mean playroom." She laughed and pointed to the window with the missing screen. "The staircase is between those two rooms, and it doesn't have a window that I remember."

"Are you sure?" he asked.

"Pretty sure, yes. But let's check the pictures." She opened her phone's album and showed him the interior shots she'd taken in the back area of the house. The two vertical windows in the extra room, the single window in the powder room, and the staircase with no window. "See? There's no space inside that matches that window."

Glancing up at Liam, she saw her confusion mirrored in his warm, chocolate-brown eyes. "How can that be?" she asked as she swept her focus back to the house and the mystery window. "Unless—"

"We've found a house with a secret room," he finished for her.

A Note from the Editors

We hope you enjoyed another exciting volume in the Mysteries of Blackberry Valley series, published by Guideposts. For over seventy-five years, Guideposts, a nonprofit organization, has been driven by a vision of a world filled with hope. We aspire to be the voice of a trusted friend, a friend who makes you feel more hopeful and connected.

By making a purchase from Guideposts, you join our community in touching millions of lives, inspiring them to believe that all things are possible through faith, hope, and prayer. Your continued support allows us to provide uplifting resources to those in need. Whether through our communities, websites, apps, or publications, we inspire our audiences, bring them together, and comfort, uplift, entertain, and guide them. Visit us at guideposts.org to learn more.

We would love to hear from you. Write us at Guideposts, P.O. Box 5815, Harlan, Iowa 51593 or call us at (800) 932-2145. Did you love *Forged in Fire*? Leave a review for this product on guideposts.org/shop. Your feedback helps others in our community find relevant products.